CONSERVATORY CANADA™

---

### VIOLIN SYLLABUS 2000 EDITION
### Effective 1 September 2000

This Syllabus replaces all previous violin syllabi,
and will remain in effect until further notice.

---

## Violin Syllabus Committee

Eileen Kearns, St. John's, NF
Dolores Vann, Gabriola Island, BC

# Contents

# Introduction

Conservatory Canada examination programs provide a new nation-wide system for evaluation and accreditation, through core programs to encourage and assess broadly based musicianship. As well, there are innovative features (such as Mini-Lessons, Recital Assessments, and Teacher Development Assessments) that increase the options for flexibility, educational value, and meaningful and friendly interaction among teacher, student and examiner.

While this syllabus is not intended as a curriculum (that's the prerogative of the teacher), it is designed to give guidance and support to teachers and their students, with built-in opportunity where possible to serve those with broader experience or varying needs.

The clearly defined goals of an examination encourage comprehensive skill development, and offer an arms-length assessment of progress against a national standard. While the examination forms a valuable part of a total picture of musical training, it should not be considered as the entire focus of music studies. *Teachers are urged to explore a wide variety of repertoire in lessons throughout the year, and then to choose from this the pieces that will be performed in the examination.* Conservatory Canada believes that the practical examination must assess as broad a spectrum of skills and musicianship as possible. So, in addition to pieces and studies, we devote significant focus to technique, aural and sight training, oral questions, and, in the higher grades, to skills in performance of orchestral excerpts. Students trained in all these disciplines will be prepared to address with confidence whatever musical challenges await them in later life.

## List Pieces & Studies

List pieces have been chosen to give a representative sampling of composers and styles. Provision for Supplementary Pieces and Irregular Lists allow for the use of works not included in this Syllabus but which may be favourites of the teacher or student. Canadian composers are strongly represented in the lists (and are identified by asterisks), and the requirement of at least one Canadian work for each grade (starting in grade 4) will introduce students to them.

## Technique

Technical requirements, including the sequence of keys, are carefully paced to help prepare for repertoire demands in each grade. Nevertheless, we have sought to balance training needs against the realities of time limitations in the lesson and varying student commitment. Where feasible, new concepts and exercises are introduced gradually, in a few keys at first, to develop basic skills without adding extra volume of work. The natural form of the minor scale is required in the early grades as the basis of understanding harmonic and melodic forms. With scales and arpeggios, a modest review process re-visits, on a revolving basis, several keys from earlier grades to keep them current and to reduce the time spent relearning them in later grades where all keys are required.

## Viva Voce

Oral questions about pieces, titles, terms, forms, and composers in examinations up to and including Grade 8 encourage general musical knowledge and understanding of the styles and specific works performed. Written History and Theory co-requisites take over this function in Grades 9 and 10.

The Violin Syllabus Committee hopes that this graded Syllabus will serve to invite exploration of new repertoire, build musicianship skills, and provide a yardstick to measure progress from year to year.

---

# GENERAL INFORMATION & REGULATIONS

This Syllabus contains regulations and requirements for Violin examinations for Grade 1 to Grade 10.
For Associate (Teacher and Performer) Diploma and Licentiate Diploma requirements, please consult the Diploma Syllabus (1998).

## GENERAL INFORMATION

### Subjects

Examinations are offered in the following subject areas:

**Practical**

| | | | |
|---|---|---|---|
| Piano | Violin | Trumpet | Flute |
| Organ (pipe) | Viola | French Horn | Clarinet |
| Guitar (classical) | Violoncello | Trombone | Saxophone |
| Voice | | Tuba | |
| Teacher Development | | | |

**Written**

| | | |
|---|---|---|
| Theory (Rudiments) | Music History | Pedagogy |
| Theory (Harmony) | | |
| Form & Analysis | | |

### Sessions

**Practical Examinations**

The Conservatory conducts two practical examination sessions during each academic year. These examinations include most instruments and voice, and are held at centres throughout Canada (new centres may be established by arrangement with the Conservatory):

1. WINTER SESSION-          last two weeks in February

2. SPRING SESSION-          the entire month of June

*Applicants should consult the current examination form for the deadline date of the specific session for which they wish to apply.*

The Conservatory will make every effort to schedule examinations around legitimate events, such as school trips or school examinations, provided notice is given IN WRITING AT THE TIME OF APPLICATION. However, because of constraints in reserving facilities and Examiners, **this cannot be guaranteed, and by submitting an application, the candidate agrees to appear for the examination as scheduled.** Candidates entering the June examinations must understand that it is not always possible to schedule music examinations around school examinations.

Candidates will be given at least two weeks notice of the date, time and place of the practical examination. Under no circumstances are candidates or their teachers permitted to change dates or times of the scheduled examination. **Examiners are instructed not to make schedule changes unless such changes have been authorized by the Office of the Registrar.**

**Written Examinations**

The Conservatory conducts three written examination sessions during each academic year throughout Canada (new centres may be established by arrangement with the Conservatory):

    1. WINTER SESSION-          second Saturday in January

    2. SPRING SESSION-          second Saturday in May

    3. SUMMER SESSION-         third Saturday in August

*Applicants should consult the current examination form for the deadline date for the specific session for which they wish to apply and for the date and exact time of day for the examination.*

## Applications

All applications must be made using the current application form. Completed forms must be submitted in person or by mail, courier, or fax (using Visa or MasterCard) to:

        The Office of the Registrar
        Conservatory Canada
        645 Windermere Road
        London, Ontario, N5X 2P1
        Fax: (519) 433-7404
        E-mail: registrar@conservatorycanada.ca

Application forms are available from the Conservatory office in London, Ontario, from local music stores, and on-line at www.conservatorycanada.ca.

A separate application form is required for each examination. All applications must be completed neatly and accurately; applications lacking necessary information may be subject to a surcharge, or rejected. Applications must be accompanied by the correct fees and must be received by the Office of the Registrar in London, Ontario NO LATER THAN THE CLOSING DATE. Applications submitted by fax or on-line will not be accepted after the deadline date; applications submitted by mail and arriving after the deadline date will be accepted ONLY if postmarked at least two weeks prior to the application deadline.

Each partial or supplemental examination requires a new application, and partial examinations should be clearly, marked as *1st part* or *2nd part*.

## Centres

Practical examinations are conducted by fully qualified Examiners appointed by the Conservatory in those centres where the number of applicants is deemed sufficient. The Conservatory reserves the right to defer examinations until a later session in any centre where the enrollment does not warrant the visit of an Examiner, or to require the candidate to travel to the nearest viable centre. The best facilities available will be provided for examinations, in centres as close as possible to the candidate's hometown. Candidates should plan to arrive at least 15 minutes before the examination is scheduled to begin.

## Payment of Fees

The appropriate fee must be included with the completed application form. A current fee schedule appears on the application form each year. Fees may be paid by cheque, Visa or MasterCard. DO NOT SEND CASH THROUGH THE MAIL. Applications submitted by fax or on-line must use either Visa or MasterCard.

## Appeals

Queries or appeals concerning the examination procedure must be filed in writing with the Office of the Registrar within 10 days of the completion of the examination.

## Cancellations

Notice of withdrawal, for any reason, must be submitted in writing to the Office of the Registrar. Consult the current application form for refund policy regarding cancellations by the candidate before the scheduled date of the examination. No refund will be considered for notice of cancellation, for whatever reason, received after the scheduled date of the examination.

## Marking Standards

The Conservatory's standard of marking, in Grades 1-10 is as follows:

| | |
|---|---|
| First-Class Honours with Distinction | 90-100 marks |
| First-Class Honours | 80-89 marks |
| Honours | 70-79 marks |
| Pass | 60-69 marks |
| Insufficient to Pass | Below 60 marks |

## Results and Notices

All examination notices, results and certificates are normally sent to the teacher for distribution to the candidates, unless specifically requested otherwise at the time of application. Under no condition will examination results be released verbally, either in person or by telephone. Because examination marks are confidential to the teacher and candidate, results CANNOT be released to any other person.

## Transfer Credits

Transfer credit is not possible for practical subjects. However, candidates who have completed successfully equivalent examinations in Theory and History courses at recognized conservatories and/or universities may apply in writing for consideration for transfer credit. If approved, the transfer credit can be used to satisfy the co-requisite requirement for the awarding of a practical certificate. The following regulations will apply:

1) To apply for a transcript evaluation with a view to obtaining transfer credit, candidates must
   i) submit a letter of application, with the appropriate fee, to the Office of the Registrar;

   ii) arrange to have an official transcript (or letter) sent by the issuing institution **directly** to the Office of the Registrar. No application for transfer credit will be considered until the official transcript is received. Transcripts sent by the candidate are NOT acceptable.

2) Transfer credit will NOT be considered for co-requisite courses completed more than TEN years before the scheduled date of the practical examination session.

## Medals for Excellence

A Medal for Excellence will be awarded to the candidate who receives the highest mark (minimum mark of 85%) in each grade for each province for the academic year. Medals are awarded in each practical instrument area, as well as for theory, and history. To be eligible, candidates must complete the examination in one sitting, and also must have completed successfully all of the prescribed Theory and History co-requisites, if appropriate. Candidates who are considered to be professional musicians and candidates who take partial or supplemental examinations are NOT eligible for medals.

## Scholarships and Awards

### Endowed Scholarships

The annual interest earned by the Conservatory's Scholarship Endowment Fund supports over 30 scholarships each year. Scholarships range from $300 to $1,000 and must be used for music tuition with any teacher anywhere in Canada. Scholarships are awarded based on examination results, and most scholarships are available to all examination candidates at any centre. The Scholarship Endowment Funds are held in trust with and managed by the London Community Foundation and the University of Alberta. Please contact the Conservatory office for a list of current scholarships and conditions.

### Prizes and Awards

From time to time, donations are received to be given as occasional prizes and awards (usually under $300). These will be awarded as stipulated by the donor and will be presented directly to the student.

## Certificates

Certificates are awarded for all practical, theory and history examinations upon the successful completion of all requirements. For practical examinations in Grades 5 to 10, certificates will be issued subject to the completion of theory/history co-requisite requirements listed for each grade. (See Theory & History co-requisites listed below on page vi.)

## Academic Credits

Conservatory Canada examination candidates may be eligible for Secondary School curriculum credits according to the requirements as outlined by the various provincial Ministries of Education.

Candidates are strongly advised to consult with their own school officials in order to determine their eligibility in their province of residence.

## Visually Impaired or Physically Challenged Candidates

The Conservatory will make every effort to make special provisions for visually impaired or physically challenged candidates. For details, please contact the Office of the Registrar *before the closing date for applications*.

---

# REGULATIONS FOR PRACTICAL EXAMINATIONS

## Conduct of Practical Examinations

Only the Examiner, or Examiners, and the candidate will be permitted to be present in the examination room during the progress of the examination. Where piano accompanists are needed, they will be permitted in the room only for those portions for which their services are required.

Recording equipment is not permitted in the examination room.

In accordance with copyright law, photocopies of musical scores (for use by the candidate or accompanist or the examiner) are NOT permitted in the examination room unless the candidate can present written authorization from the copyright holder. The examiner has been instructed NOT to proceed with the examination while unauthorized photocopies are present.

Candidates must list in the appropriate place on the back of the examination notice all repertoire to be performed in the examination. This list must be given to the examiner at the start of the examination.

## Editions

Any standard edition of the music may be used for the examination. However, candidates are encouraged to choose editions that represent the composer's intentions in the clearest and most straightforward manner. Candidates may NOT use simplified or adapted versions of works to be performed.

## Irregular Lists

Any piece not found in the list pieces for the particular grade in this syllabus constitutes an irregular list piece.

Candidates may make written request, by mail, fax or in person, to the Office of the Registrar for approval to perform a maximum of ONE irregular list piece.

Requests for approval must include full details of the piece along with a copy of the music, and must reach the Registrar's Office at least 30 days before the deadline for application. The Conservatory cannot take responsibility if the request is denied and the piece deemed inappropriate for the examination.

For those pieces given special approval, an official form setting this out will be sent to the candidate who must, in turn, hand it along with the printed score to the Examiner at the time of the examination.

A piece approved as an irregular list piece may not be played at a subsequent examination.

*NOTE: It is permissible, without special approval, to include one piece from the next higher grade in this Syllabus, providing it is from the same list. Compositions listed in this Syllabus for more than one grade higher may NOT be used.*

## Partial Examinations

Candidates in Grades 7, 8, 9 and 10 may choose to take the examination in two parts, each at a different session. These partial examinations are to be divided into two reasonably equals parts, each part comprising approximately 50% of the marks allotted for that grade (see MARKS at the end of each grade). The first part must contain no less than 44% and no more than 56% of the requirements. The second part must be completed within twelve months following the first sitting, and must include all aspects not previously examined in the first part.

The division of the examination is left to the discretion of the teacher and candidate. Sections given a composite mark (*e.g.* the complete technical requirements or the complete aural tests) may not be sub-divided and must be completed at one sitting. At each sitting the list presented to the Examiner must contain details of all components that are to be heard. Each section as it is presented will be awarded a mark.

No portion of a partial examination completed during the first sitting may be repeated for the second sitting in order to attempt to improve the mark already awarded.

The total mark at the conclusion of the second sitting determines the standing of the candidate, and there can be no recourse to adjustment of this final mark. If the results of the first sitting are low, then it might be to the advantage of the candidate to start over.

Candidates who choose to play a partial examination will not be eligible for either scholarships or medals.

## Theory & History Co-requisites for Practical Certificates

Theoretical subjects are required for practical Certificates for all instruments and voice beyond Grade 4. Certificates are issued only when the required Theory and/or History co-requisites are completed. Candidates are strongly urged to complete all written co-requisites before entering for the practical examination. Co-requisites must be successfully completed within ten years of completion of the practical examinations. No certificate will be awarded after this period has lapsed.

It is recognized that, in some cases, Western Ontario Conservatory and/or Western Board courses do not have exactly the same content as the Conservatory Canada equivalent. Nevertheless, in the interest of convenience and fairness, the equivalents (along with the various written co-requisites for each grade in all instruments and voice) given below will be considered as having covered the same material.

Candidates who have completed successfully Theory and History examinations at the August 1998 session or earlier under either The Western Board syllabus or Western Ontario Conservatory syllabus may use these equivalent credits to satisfy the co-requisites for the awarding of a practical certificate as outlined in this syllabus.

For details concerning regulations and requirements for all Rudiments/Theory and History examinations, candidates should consult the new *Theory & History Syllabus (1998)*. This syllabus must be used beginning with the January 1999 written examination session.

## Mini-Lessons

Mini-Lessons provide a unique learning opportunity for students at all grade levels and, at the same time, serve as an informal, private workshop for the teacher. It is an optional 15-minute private lesson, with the teacher present, to be given by the examiner immediately following the practical examination. The Mini-Lesson will not be used to review any aspect of the candidate's performance in the preceding examination, but rather it may be used to explore ways to overcome particular technical difficulties or investigate ideas concerning musicianship and style relating to proposed new pieces or studies to help the candidate prepare for the next year. Mini-Lessons are tailored to the needs of the student, and to this end, the teacher and/or the student may wish to suggest to the examiner what they would like to cover in the Mini-Lesson. Candidates wishing to register for a Mini-Lesson should indicate this in the appropriate place on the examination application form and also enclose the appropriate Mini-Lesson fee.

# INSTRUCTIONS FOR VIOLIN CANDIDATES

1.  For those grades where a separate mark is given for memory, full marks will be awarded only when each of the pieces is memorized accurately. Full marks will not be awarded for performances that need re-starts or include stumbles or for performances where the musical score is used. Candidates are required to memorize all List Pieces and the prescribed technical requirements (see the technique section for the specific grade). In Grade 10, where a separate mark is not given for memory, candidates can expect a deduction of up to 10% for work that is not properly memorized.

2.  Candidates in *Grades 1-4 inclusive* must play ALL repeats. No repeats are to be played in Grades 5-10 unless they are essential to the musical sense of the piece (*e.g.* a Baroque dance or a Classical minuet & trio). However, *Da Capo* and *Dal Segno* indications must always be observed.

3.  Metronome markings are given in each grade for the performance of the various technical tests. These speeds should be regarded as minimum tempi.

4.  The candidate must provide the examiner with an original printed copy of all pieces to be performed.

5.  In Grades 1 to 5 inclusive, the teacher or accompanist may tune the candidate's instrument before the examination begins. The examiner must not be asked to do so. From Grades 6 to 10, tuning is considered an essential part of performance and candidates are expected to tune their own instruments.

6.  Candidates must provide their own music stand for examinations.

7.  Candidates are asked to consider time limitations when choosing repertoire for their examination. The total examination time is listed at the beginning of each grade, and all aspects of the examination must be covered within this time frame. In each grade, list pieces, studies and a supplementary piece make up approximately 50% of the marks, and therefore performance time should be approximately 50% of the examination time.


## Publications

While there are many textbooks available that can be used to prepare for examinations in aural, sight reading and *viva voce* sections, candidates should check carefully all requirements in this Syllabus well in advance of the examination.


**Candidates are expected to know all of the current regulations and requirements for the examinations as outlined in this Syllabus. No allowance can be made for candidates who misread or fail to follow any of the regulations and/or requirements for the examination.**

---

# GRADE ONE

Length of the examination: 20 minutes

Examination Fee: Please consult the current examination application form for the schedule of fees.

Co-requisite: None. There is NO written examination co-requisite for the awarding of the Grade 1 Practical Certificate.

## Requirements & Marking

| Requirement | Total Marks |
|---|---|
| TWO LIST PIECES | |
| Piece #1 | 16 |
| Piece #2 | 16 |
| TWO STUDIES (6 marks each) | 12 |
| ONE SUPPLEMENTARY PIECE | 8 |
| TECHNICAL TESTS | |
| Scales & Arpeggios | 16 |
| SIGHT READING | |
| Rhythm Pattern | 3 |
| Playing | 7 |
| AURAL TESTS | 10 |
| VIVA VOCE | 8 |
| MARKS FOR MEMORY | |
| List pieces only (2 marks each) | 4 |
| TOTAL POSSIBLE MARKS | 100 |

*NOTE: The examination program must include at least ONE work by a Canadian composer. The Canadian work may be chosen from the List Pieces OR as the Supplementary Piece. Candidates who fail to include a Canadian work will be subject to an automatic deduction from their over-all total mark.*

## Pieces

Candidates must be prepared to play TWO pieces from the list below, chosen to contrast in style, key, tempo, etc. Your choice must include TWO different composers. All pieces requiring accompaniment must be played with accompaniment. All pieces were available in print at the time the syllabus was prepared. Although suggested editions have been given below to assist candidates in identifying and purchasing music, ANY STANDARD EDITION may be used for the examination.

> \* = *Canadian composer*

**ARBEAU**
Les Bouffans (*Arbeau's Orchesography*)    Faber
  (*The Young Violinist's Repertoire Book 1*)
**\*ARCHER, V.**
  *Twelve Miniatures*    Waterloo
  Choose ANY ONE of
  No. 2 A Quiet Song
  No. 3 On Tip Toe

**BACH, J. S.**
March in A (*Peasant's Cantata*)    Faber
  (*The Young Violinist's Repertoire Book 1*)
Minuet in G, BWV Anh. 114    Any edition
**BARTOK, B.**
Teasing Song (*Doflein Method, Vol. 1*)    Schott

**BAYLY, I.**

| | |
|---|---|
| Long, Long Ago (in A) | Summy Birchard |
| (*Suzuki Violin School, Vol. 1*) | |

**BLAIR, D.**

| | |
|---|---|
| Marching Bands | CMC |

**CORRETTE, M.**

| | |
|---|---|
| Fanfare (*The Young Violinist's Repertoire Book I*) | Faber |
| Minuet (*Doflein Method, Vol. 1*) | Schott |

**\*COULTHARD, J.**

| | |
|---|---|
| The Great Elephant (*Encore Series Book I*) | Harris |
| Grandfather Tells a Witch Story (*Encore Series, Book 1*) | Harris |
| The Sailboat on the Lake (*Encore Series, Book 1*) | Harris |

**\*DUKE, D.**

| | |
|---|---|
| All Alone (*Encore Series, Book 1*) | Harris |
| The Alligator (*Encore Series, Book 1*) | Harris |

**\*ETHRIDGE, J.**

| | |
|---|---|
| Homage to Bartok (*Encore Series, Book 1*) | Harris |
| The Lonely Mermaid (*Encore Series, Book 1*) | Harris |

**\*FLEMING, R.**

| | |
|---|---|
| Scotty Lad (*Encore Series Book I*) | Harris |

**FOLK**

| | |
|---|---|
| \*Alouette (*Folk Fiddle Playtime*) | Faber |
| Early One Morning (*Folk Fiddle Playtime*) | Faber |
| May Song (*Suzuki Violin School, Vol. 1*) | Summy Birchard |
| O Come Little Children | Summy Birchard |
| (*Suzuki Violin School, Vol. 1*) | |
| Wiegenlied aus Tirol (*Folk Fiddle Playtime*) | Faber |

**HÄNDEL, G. F.**

| | |
|---|---|
| March from "Judas Maccabeus" | Faber |
| (*The Young Violinist's Repertoire Book I*) | |

**HAYDN, F. J.**

| | |
|---|---|
| Andante (*The Young Violinist's Repertoire Book I*) | Faber |

**\*HYSLOP, R.**

| | |
|---|---|
| Autumn Parade (*Music Stands*) | Harris |
| Rapido (*Music Stands*) | Harris |
| Roumanian Dance (*Music Stands*) | Harris |
| T.V. Theme (*Music Stands*) | Harris |

**KABELEVSKY, D.**

| | |
|---|---|
| Games (*20 Pieces for Violin and Piano, Op. 80*) | MCA (Leeds) |
| March (*20 Pieces for Violin and Piano, Op. 80*) | MCA (Leeds) |
| Waltz (*20 Pieces for Violin and Piano, Op. 80*) | MCA (Leeds) |

**DE KEYSER, P.**

| | |
|---|---|
| Hungarian Dance (*Violin Playtime Book I*) | Faber |
| Poëme (*Violin Playtime Book I*) | Faber |
| The Bells (*Violin Playtime Book I*) | Faber |

**KOMAROVSKY, I.**

| | |
|---|---|
| The Grey Dove (*The Young Violinist's Repertoire Book I*) | Faber |

**KRASEV, A.**

| | |
|---|---|
| Pony Trot (*The Young Violinist's Repertoire Book I*) | Faber |

**PURCELL, H.**

| | |
|---|---|
| Rigadoon (*Classical Album of Early Grade Pieces*) | Boston |

**SUZUKI, S.**

| | |
|---|---|
| Allegro in A (*Suzuki Violin School, Vol. 1*) | Summy Birchard |
| Allegretto in D (*Suzuki Violin School, Vol. 1*) | Summy Birchard |
| Andantino in D (*Suzuki Violin School, Vol. 1*) | Summy Birchard |

**SZELENYI, I.**

| | |
|---|---|
| Playsong (*24 Little Concert Pieces*) | Boosey & Hawkes |

## Studies

Candidates must be prepared to play TWO contrasting studies in different keys from the following list. Memorization is recommended although NOT required.

**DE KEYSER, P.**

| | |
|---|---|
| *Violin Playtime Studies* | Faber |
| Choose ANY ONE of | |
| Nos. 2, 3, 11 | |

**DOFLEIN, E.**

| | |
|---|---|
| *Doflein Method – Volume 1* | Schott |
| No. 36 | |

**KINSEY, H.**

| | |
|---|---|
| *Elem. & Progressive Studies for Violin* | Assoc. Board of RSM |
| Choose ANY ONE of | |
| Nos. 2, 4, 5, 7 | |

**SANDOR, ET AL**

| | |
|---|---|
| *Violin Tutor I* | Editio Musica Budapest |
| No. 60 | |

**SUZUKI, S.**

| | |
|---|---|
| *Suzuki Violin School – Volume 1* | Summy Birchard |
| Perpetual Motion in A or D | |

♪ "singles" and ♫ 'doubles"

Etude ♪ only

**WOOF, R.**

| | |
|---|---|
| *Fifty Elementary Studies for Violin* | Assoc. Board of RSM |
| Choose ANY ONE of | |
| Nos. 1, 3, 5, 6 | |

## Supplementary Piece

Candidates must be prepared to play ONE Supplementary Piece. This piece need not be from the Syllabus lists, and may be chosen entirely at the discretion of the teacher and student. It may represent a period or style of piece not already included in the examination program, but which holds special interest for the candidate. The choice must be within the following guidelines:

1) The equivalent level of difficulty of the piece may be at a higher grade level, providing it is within the technical and musical grasp of the candidate.

2) Pieces at the pre-grade 1 level are acceptable.

3) The piece must be for solo violin (with or without piano accompaniment). Duets and trios are not acceptable.

4) Candidates with exceptional talent for improvisation may wish to improvise upon a theme of their choice. In this case, items 1 and 2 (above) will apply. Marks will be given for originality, musical inventiveness, and structural unity.

Special approval is not required for the Supplementary Piece. However, poor suitability of the choice may be reflected in the mark. Memorization is encouraged, although NOT required.

## Technical Tests

All technical tests must be played from memory, evenly, with good tone, secure intonation, with all of the listed bowings, ascending and descending in the keys stated.

### SCALES
*ALL scales to be played from memory, ascending AND descending.*

|  | Keys | Octaves | Note Values | M.M. ♩= | Bowings | Comments |
|---|---|---|---|---|---|---|
| Major | A, D | 1 | ♩ | 72 | detaché | Tonic may be doubled in value for G scale only (see example) |
|  | G | 2 | ♩ | 60 | detaché |  |
| Natural Minor | e | 1 | ♩ | 72 | detaché | Start on D string |

### ARPEGGIOS
*ALL arpeggios to be played from memory, ascending AND descending. Do NOT repeat the top note.*

|  | Keys | Octaves | Note Values | M.M. ♩= | Bowings | Comments |
|---|---|---|---|---|---|---|
| Major | A, D | 1 | ♩ | 72 | detaché |  |
|  | G | 2 | ♩ | 60 | detaché |  |
| Minor | e | 1 | ♩ | 72 | detaché | Start on D string |

Example: G major scale (2 octaves) – either pattern may be played, at the candidate's choice.

## Sight Reading

Candidates are required to perform at sight a) a rhythmic exercise and b) a passage of violin score as described below. The candidate will be given a brief period to scan the score, but not to "practise silently" before beginning to play. Candidates must perform each section without counting aloud. It is recommended that candidates maintain a steady beat, and avoid the unnecessary repetition caused by attempting to correct errors during the performance.

| a) Rhythm | | b) Violin Passage | |
|---|---|---|---|
| To tap, clap or play on one note (at the candidate's choice) a simple rhythm. | | To play at sight a simple melody, within the limits of the treble staff. | |
| Length | 4 bars | Keys | D Major |
| Time signature | 2/4, 3/4 | Length | 4 bars |
| Note values | dotted 1/2, 1/2, 1/4, 1/8 | Time signature | 2/4, 3/4 |
| Rest values | no rest values | Note values | dotted 1/2, 1/2, 1/4 |
| | | Rest values | whole rest |

Example: a) Rhythm

Example: b) Violin passage

## Aural Tests

The candidate will be required:

i) to clap back the rhythmic pattern of a short melody, 4 bars in length, in 2/4 or 4/4 time, consisting of half, dotted half, quarter and eighth notes, after it has been played twice by the Examiner at the keyboard. Following is the approximate level of difficulty:

ii) to identify *major* or *minor* triad chords played once by the Examiner in broken form; in close, root position

iii) the *major* common [four-note] chord of any key will be played once by the Examiner in broken form slowly, ascending and descending. The chord will be in root position. One of the four notes will then be re-sounded for the candidate to identify by saying, at the candidate's choice:

| EITHER | its interval number [1, 3, 5, 8] |
|---|---|
| OR | its tonic sol-fa name [doh, me, sol, upper doh]. |

## Viva Voce

Candidates must be prepared to give verbal answers to questions on the TWO List pieces selected for the examination. Candidates must ensure that all teaching notes and other written comments are removed from the score before the examination. The questions will include the following elements:

i) to find and explain all of the signs (including clefs, time signatures, key signatures, accidentals, etc.), articulation markings (legato, staccato, accents, phrase or slur markings, etc.), dynamic and tempo markings, and other musical terms and signs as they may be found in the two selected pieces.

ii) without reference to the score, to give the title, key and composer of the piece.

iii) to explain the meaning of the title of the piece.

---

# GRADE TWO

Length of the examination:    20 minutes

Examination Fee:    Please consult the current examination application form for the schedule of fees.

Co-requisite:    None. There is NO written examination co-requisite for the awarding of the Grade 2 Practical Certificate.

## Requirements & Marking

| Requirement | Total Marks |
|---|---|
| TWO LIST PIECES | |
| Piece #1 | 16 |
| Piece #2 | 16 |
| TWO STUDIES (6 marks each) | 12 |
| ONE SUPPLEMENTARY PIECE | 8 |
| TECHNICAL TESTS | |
| Scales &Arpeggios | 16 |
| SIGHT READING | |
| Rhythm Pattern | 3 |
| Playing | 7 |
| AURAL TESTS | 10 |
| VIVA VOCE | 8 |
| MARKS FOR MEMORY | |
| List pieces only (2 marks each) | 4 |
| TOTAL POSSIBLE MARKS | 100 |

*NOTE: The examination program must include at least ONE work by a Canadian composer. The Canadian work may be chosen from the List Pieces OR as the Supplementary Piece. Candidates who fail to include a Canadian work will be subject to an automatic deduction from their over-all total mark.*

## Pieces

Candidates must be prepared to play TWO pieces from the list below, chosen to contrast in style, key, tempo, etc. Your choice must include TWO different composers. All pieces requiring accompaniment must be played with accompaniment. All pieces were available in print at the time the syllabus was prepared. Although suggested editions have been given below to assist candidates in identifying and purchasing music, ANY STANDARD EDITION may be used for the examination.

*  = Canadian composer

**\*ARCHER, V.**
*Twelve Miniatures*                                          Waterloo
  Choose ANY ONE of
  No. 1 Jig
  No. 9 Lullaby
**BACH, J. S.**
  Minuet No. 2 (*Suzuki Violin School, Vol. 1*)    Summy Birchard
  Minuet No. 3 (*Suzuki Violin School, Vol. 1*)    Summy Birchard
  Musette from *English Suite in G minor*, BWV808 Summy Birchard
    (*Suzuki Violin School, Vol. 2*)

**\*BECKWITH, J.**
  Reel 1 (*Eight Miniatures*)                              Harris
**\*BARNES, M.**
  Folk Dance (*Three Folk Dances, No. 2*)              CMC
**BRAHMS, J.**
  Folk Song (*First Solo Pieces for Violin & Piano*)    Schott
  The Hunter (*First Solo Pieces for Violin & Piano*)   Schott
  Waltz (*Suzuki Violin School, Vol. 2*)      Summy Birchard

CHEDERVILLE, E.-P.
  Gavotte in A (*The Young Violinist's Repertoire Book II*)    Faber
*COULTHARD, J.
  A Little Sorrow (*Encore Series, Book II*)    Harris
  A Quiet Moment (*Encore Series, Book I*)    Harris
ELGAR, E.
  *Six Easy Pieces, Op. 22*    Any edition
  Choose ANY ONE of
  Nos. 1, 2, 4
  Allegretto (*The Young Violinist's Repertoire Book II*)    Faber
*ETHRIDGE, J.
  Morris Dance (*Encore Series, Book I*)    Harris
  The Subway Train (*Encore Series, Book I*)    Harris
*FLEMING, R.
  Singer Man    Harris
*FOLK, CANADIAN (ARR. DUKE)
  Un canadien errant (*Encore Series, Book II*)    Harris
*FOLK, CANADIAN (ARR. MCLEAN)
  Vive la canadienne    Harris
GABRIELI, D.
  Ploughman's Song (*First Solo Pieces for Violin & Piano*)    Schott
GRETCHANINOFF, A.
  Morning Stroll (*First Solo Pieces for Violin & Piano*)    Schott
  The Jester (*First Solo Pieces for Violin & Piano*)    Schott
HÄNDEL, G. F.
  Bourée (*Suzuki Violin School, Vol. 2*)    Summy Birchard
  *Classical Album of Early Grade Pieces*    Boston
  Choose ANY ONE of
  Minuet No. 7 in D minor
  Minuet No. 8 in F

*HYSLOP, R.
  Reverie (*Music Stands*)    Harris
  Violin valentine (*Music Stands*)    Harris
KABALEVSKY, D.
  *Twenty Pieces for Violin & Piano, Op. 80*    Leeds (Can.)
  Choose ANY ONE of
  No. 6 A Song
  No. 8 Skipping and Hopping
*MCDOUGALL, B.
  Tall Ships    Harris
MOZART, W. A.
  Lied (*The Young Violinist's Repertoire Book II*)    Faber
  Allegro (*Classical Album of Early Grade Pieces*)    Boston
NELSON, S.
  *Piece by Piece 2*    Boosey & Hawkes
  Choose ANY TWO of
  Henry's Hornpipe
  Willow Water
  Hurry on Down
  Jingling Jimmy
RAICHEV, A.
  Shepherd's Song (*The Young Violinist's Repertoire Book I*)    Faber
REINECKE, C.
  Ländler (*The Young Violinist's Repertoire Book I*)    Faber
SCHUBERT, F.
  Landler (*Classical Album of Early Grade Pieces*)    Boston
  Waltz (*Classical Album of Early Grade Pieces*)    Boston
SCHUMANN, R.
  Happy Farmer (*Suzuki Violin School, Vol. 1*)    Summy Birchard

# Studies

Candidates must be prepared to play TWO contrasting studies in different keys from the following list. Memorization is recommended although NOT required.

DE KEYSER, P.
  *Violin Playtime Studies*    Faber
  Choose ANY ONE of
  Nos. 17, 21, 22, 23
KINSEY, H.
  *Elem. & Progressive Studies for Violin*    Assoc. Board of RSM
  Choose ANY ONE of
  Nos. 9, 10, 11, 12, 13, 14, 15, 16
SUZUKI, S.
  *Suzuki Violin School – Volume 2*    Summy Birchard
  Long, Long Ago, with Variation

WOHLFAHRT, F.
  *Sixty Studies for Violin Op. 45 Book 1*    Schirmer
  Choose ANY ONE of
  Nos. 1, 2, 3, 4
WOOF, R.
  *Fifty Elementary Studies for Violin*    Assoc. Board of RSM
  Choose ANY ONE of
  Nos. 9, 11, 12, 13, 15

# Supplementary Piece

Candidates must be prepared to play ONE Supplementary Piece. This piece need not be from the Syllabus lists, and may be chosen entirely at the discretion of the teacher and student. It may represent a period or style of piece not already included in the examination program, but which holds special interest for the candidate. The choice must be within the following guidelines:

1)  The equivalent level of difficulty of the piece may be at a higher grade level, providing it is within the technical and musical grasp of the candidate.

2)  Pieces below the equivalent of Grade 1 level are not acceptable.

3)  The piece must be for solo violin (with or without piano accompaniment). Duets and trios are not acceptable.

4) Candidates with exceptional talent for improvisation may wish to improvise on a theme of their choice. In this case, items 1 and 2 (above) will apply. Marks will be given for originality, musical inventiveness, and structural unity.

Special approval is not required for the Supplementary Piece. However, poor suitability of the choice may be reflected in the mark. Memorization is encouraged, although NOT required.

## Technical Tests

All technical tests must be played from memory, evenly, with good tone, secure intonation, with all of the listed bowings, ascending and descending, in the keys stated.

### SCALES
*ALL scales to be played from memory, ascending AND descending.*

| | Keys | Octaves | Note Values | M.M. ♩= | Bowings | Comments |
|---|---|---|---|---|---|---|
| Major | E♭, F, C<br><br>A, B♭ | 1<br><br>2 | ♩ | 66 | detaché<br>**or**<br>♩⌣♩ | Tonic may be doubled in value; see p. 3 for example |
| Natural Minor | a, d | 1 | ♩ | 66 | detaché | a from A string;<br>d from D string |
| Melodic Minor | a, d | 1 | ♩ | 66 | detaché | a from A string;<br>d from D string |

### ARPEGGIOS
*ALL arpeggios to be played from memory, ascending AND descending. Do NOT repeat the top note.*

| | Keys | Octaves | Note Values | M.M. ♩= | Bowings | Comments |
|---|---|---|---|---|---|---|
| Major | E♭, F, C<br><br>A, B♭ | 1<br><br>2 | ♩ | 66 | detaché<br>**or**<br>♩ ♩ ♩ | |
| Minor | a, d | 1 | ♩ | 66 | detaché | a from A string<br>d from D string |

## Sight Reading

Candidates are required to perform at sight a) a rhythmic exercise and b) a passage of violin score as described below. The candidate will be given a brief period to scan the score, but not to "practise silently" before beginning to play. Candidates must perform each section without counting aloud. It is recommended that candidates choose a moderate tempo, maintain a steady beat, and avoid the unnecessary repetition caused by attempting to correct errors during the performance.

| *a) Rhythm* | | *b) Violin Passage* | |
|---|---|---|---|
| To tap, clap or play on one note (at the candidate's choice) a simple rhythm. | | To play at sight a simple melody, within the range of D-E$^1$, treble clef | |
| Length | 4 bars | Keys | C, G, D Major |
| Time signature | 3/4, 4/4 | Length | 4 bars |
| Note values | dotted 1/2, 1/2, 1/4, 1/8, & dotted 1/4 followed by 1/8 | Time signature | 2/4, 3/4, 4/4 |
| | | Note values | dotted 1/2, 1/2, 1/4, 1/8 |
| Rest values | whole, 1/2. ¼ | Rest values | whole, 1/2 |

Example: a) Rhythm

Example: b) Violin Passage

## Aural Tests

The candidate will be required:

i) to clap back the rhythmic pattern of a short melody in 3/4 or 4/4 time, consisting of half, dotted half, quarter, dotted quarter and eighth notes, after it has been played twice by the Examiner at the keyboard. Following is the approximate level of difficulty:

ii) to identify *major* or *minor* triad chords played once by the Examiner in broken form and in close, root position.

iii) to identify *major* or *harmonic minor* scales played once by the Examiner, ascending and descending, at a moderately slow tempo.

iv) the *major* common [four-note] chord of any key will be played once by the Examiner in broken form slowly, ascending and descending. The chord will be in root position. One of the four notes will then be re-sounded for the candidate to identify, by saying, at the candidate's choice:

EITHER          its interval number [1, 3, 5, 8]
OR               its tonic sol-fa name [doh, me, soh, upper doh].

## Viva Voce

Candidates must be prepared to verbal answers to questions on the TWO List pieces selected for the examination. Candidates must ensure that all teaching notes and other written comments are removed from the score before the examination. The questions will include the following elements:

i) to find and explain all of the signs (including clefs, time signatures, key signatures, accidentals, etc.), articulation markings (legato, staccato, accents, phrase or slur markings, etc.), dynamic and tempo markings, and other musical terms as they may be found in the two selected pieces.

ii) without reference to the score, to give the title, key and composer of the piece.

iii) to explain the meaning of the title of the piece.

---

# GRADE THREE

Length of the examination:  20 minutes

Examination Fee:  Please consult the current examination application form for the schedule of fees.

Co-requisite:  None. There is NO written examination co-requisite for the awarding of the Grade 3 Practical Certificate.

## Requirements & Marking

| Requirement | Total Marks |
|---|---|
| TWO LIST PIECES | |
| Piece #1 | 16 |
| Piece #2 | 16 |
| TWO STUDIES | |
| One from Study List A | 6 |
| One from Study List B | 6 |
| ONE SUPPLEMENTARY PIECE | 8 |
| TECHNICAL TESTS | |
| Scales & Arpeggios | 16 |
| SIGHT READING | |
| Rhythm Pattern | 3 |
| Playing | 7 |
| AURAL TESTS | 10 |
| VIVA VOCE | 8 |
| MARKS FOR MEMORY | |
| List pieces only (2 marks each) | 4 |
| TOTAL POSSIBLE MARKS | 100 |

*NOTE: The examination program must include at least ONE work by a Canadian composer. The Canadian work may be chosen from the List Pieces OR as the Supplementary Piece. Candidates who fail to include a Canadian work will be subject to an automatic deduction from their over-all total mark.*

## Pieces

Candidates must be prepared to play TWO pieces from the list below, chosen to contrast in style, key, tempo, etc. Your choice must include TWO different composers. All pieces requiring accompaniment must be played with accompaniment. All pieces were available in print at the time the syllabus was prepared. Although suggested editions have been given below to assist candidates in identifying and purchasing music, ANY STANDARD EDITION may be used for the examination.

*   * = Canadian composer*

**\*ARCHER, V.**
*Twelve Miniatures*  Waterloo
Choose ANY ONE of
No. 7 In Church
No. 8 Joyous
No. 11 Sunny Skies
The Dancing Kitten  CMC
*(Sherburne G. McCurdy Festival Series)*
**BACH, J. S.**
March in D BWV Anh.122 (*10 Little Classics for Violin*)  Boston

**(BACH, J. S. CONT.)**
Minuet BWV 114 & 115 (*Suzuki Vln. School, Vol. 3*)   S. Birchard
Gavotte in G minor BWV 822           Summy Birchard
(*Suzuki Violin School, Vol. 3*)
**\*BECKWITH, J.**
Reel 2 *(Eight Miniatures)*           Harris
**BEETHOVEN, L. VAN**
Menuetto and Trio (*Serenade for String Trio, Op. 8*)   Schott
(*First Solo Pieces for Violin & Piano*)
**\*BLAIR, D.**
Hoedown           CMC
**DE BERIOT, C. (ARR. CORDER)**
Rondo (*An Evening of Violin Classics*)           Schirmer
**\*COULTHARD, J.**
Under the Sea (*Encore Series, Book IV*)           Harris
Friend Squirrel (*Encore Series, Book III*)           Harris
**DANBÉ, J.**
Menuet in D (*First Solo Pieces for Violin & Piano*)           Schott
**DANCLA, C.**
Mazurka Op. 123, No. 11 (*An Evening of Violin Classics*) Schirmer
Serenade Op. 48, No. 13 (*An Evening of Violin Classics*)   Schirmer
**DIABELLI, A.**
Andante Cantabile           Schott
**\*DUKE, D.**
Motorcycles (*Encore Series, Book II*)           Harris
Pibroch: In Folksong Style (*Encore Series, Book II*)           Harris
**DVORAK, A.**
Humoresque (*Suzuki Violin School, Vol. 3*)           Summy Birchard
**ELGAR, E.**
*Six Easy Pieces*           Boswell
Choose ANY ONE of
Nos. 3, 5, 6
**\*FLEMING, R.**
Whistler's Tune           CMC
Berceuse           CMC
**FOLK (ARR. BECKWITH)**
Ye Banks and Braes (*Eight Miniatures*)           Harris
**GOSSEC, F. J.**
Gavotte in G (*Suzuki Violin School, Vol. 1*)           Summy Birchard
**GRETCHANINOFF, A.**
The Joker (*The Young Violinist's Repertoire Book III*)           Faber
**GRIEG, E.**
Solvejg's Song (*Peer Gynt*) (*Universal Geigen Album I*)   Universal

**HASSE, J. A.**
Bourée AND Minuet           Schott
(*First Solo Pieces for Violin & Piano*)
**\*HEINS, D.**
The Bellboy Suite           Harris
**HENRY, J. H.**
Danse de Village           Bosworth
**\*HYSLOP, R.**
Rainstorm (*Music Stands*)           Harris
Tennis Game (*Music Stands*)           Harris
On the Mark (*Music Stands*)           Harris
**KABALEVSKY, D.**
*20 Pieces for Violin and Piano, Op. 80*           Leeds (Can.)
Choose ANY ONE of
No. 13 Polka
No. 14 Melody
**KROLL, W.**
Donkey Doodle           Schirmer
**LULLY, J. B.**
Gavotte in A minor (*Suzuki Violin School, Vol. 2*)   Summy Birchard
**MOZART, W. A.**
Minuet and Trio, K.1 (*First Solo Pieces for Violin & Piano*)   Schott
**PAGANINI, N.**
Theme from "Witches Dance"           Summy Birchard
(*Suzuki Violin School, Vol. 2*)
**PORTNOFF**
Minuet in the Old Style           Fischer
**SCHUBERT, F.**
Andante (*String Quartet in A minor*)           Schott
(*First Solo Pieces for Violin & Piano*)
Minuet and Trio (*Symphony No. 5*)           Schott
(*First Solo Pieces for Violin & Piano*)
**SCHUMANN, R.**
Two Grenadiers (*Suzuki Violin School, Vol. 2*)   Summy Birchard
**SEVERN, E.**
Perpetuum Mobile           Fischer
**TCHAIKOVSKY, P. I.**
Sharmanka (*The Young Violinist's Repertoire Book II*)           Faber
**TELEMANN, G. P.**
Andante & Allegro (*First Solo Pieces for Violin & Piano*)   Schott
**TROTT, J.**
Puppet Show           Schirmer
**WHITTAKER, J. (ARR. BECKWITH)**
Darby O'Kelly (*Eight Miniatures*)           Harris

# Studies

Candidates must be prepared to play TWO contrasting studies in different keys, ONE from Study List A and ONE from Study List B, below. Memorization is recommended although not required.

### STUDY LIST A

**DE KEYSER, P.**
*Violin Study Time*           Faber
Choose ANY ONE of
Nos. 2, 4, 7, 8, 9
**WOHLFAHRT, F.**
*Sixty Studies for Violin, Op. 45, Book 1*           Schirmer
Choose ANY ONE of
Nos. 6, 9, 11, 16

**DE KAYSER, P.**
*Elem. & Progressive Studies for Violin,, Op. 20, Book 1* Schirmer
Choose ANY ONE of
Nos. 1, 2

### STUDY LIST B

**WOHLFAHRT, F.**
*Sixty Studies for Violin, Op. 45, Book 2*           Schirmer
Choose ANY ONE of
Nos. 31, 33, 34 (omit articulations)

# Supplementary Piece

Candidates must be prepared to play ONE Supplementary Piece. This piece need not be from the Syllabus lists, and may be chosen entirely at the discretion of the teacher and student. It may represent a period or style of piece not already included in the examination program, but which holds special interest for the candidate. The choice must be within the following guidelines:

1) The equivalent level of difficulty of the piece may be at a higher grade level, providing it is within the technical and musical grasp of the candidate.

2) Pieces below the equivalent of Grade 2 level are not acceptable.

3) The piece must be for solo violin (with or without piano accompaniment). Duets and trios are not acceptable.

4) Candidates with exceptional talent for improvisation may wish to improvise on a theme of their choice. In this case, items 1 and 2 (above) will apply. Marks will be given for originality, musical inventiveness, and structural unity.

Special approval is not required for the Supplementary Piece. However, poor suitability of the choice may be reflected in the mark. Memorization is encouraged, although NOT required.

# Technical Tests

All technical tests must be played from memory, evenly, with good tone, secure intonation, with all of the listed bowing, ascending and descending, in the keys stated.

## SCALES
*ALL scales to be played from memory, ascending AND descending.*

| | Keys | Octaves | Note Values | M.M. ♩= | Bowings | Comments |
|---|---|---|---|---|---|---|
| Major | A♭, B<br><br>C | 2 | ♪<br><br>♩ | 72 | ♫♫ *detaché* | C played ALL in 2nd *or* ALL in 3rd position |
| Melodic Minor | g, a | 2 | ♩ | 72 | detaché | |
| Harmonic Minor | g, a | 2 | ♩ | 72 | detaché | |

## ARPEGGIOS
*ALL arpeggios to be played from memory, ascending AND descending. Do NOT repeat the top note.*

| | Keys | Octaves | Note Values | M.M. ♩= | Bowings | Comments |
|---|---|---|---|---|---|---|
| Major | A♭, B, C | 2 | ♫♩ ³ | 60 | detaché | C played ALL in 2nd *or* ALL in 3rd position |
| Minor | g, a | 2 | ♫♩ ³ | 60 | detaché | |

# Sight Reading

Candidates are required to perform at sight a) a rhythmic exercise and b) a passage of violin score as described below. The candidate will be given a brief period to scan the score, but not to "practise silently" before beginning to play. Candidates must perform each section without counting aloud. It is recommended that candidates maintain a steady beat, and avoid the unnecessary repetition caused by attempting to correct errors during the performance.

| a) Rhythm | | b) Violin Passage | |
|---|---|---|---|
| To tap or play on one note (at the candidate's choice) a simple rhythm. | | To play at sight a simple melody, within the range of D-F#¹, treble clef. | |
| Length | 4 bars | Keys | C, G, D, F Major & a minor |
| Time signature | 2/4, 3/4, 4/4 | Length | 4 bars |
| Note values | whole, 1/2, dotted 1/2, 1/4. 1/8, & dotted 1/4 followed by 1/8 | Time signature | 2/4, 3/4, 4/4 |
| | | Note values | whole. dotted 1/2, 1/2, 1/4, 1/8 |
| Rest values | whole, 1/2, 1/4. 1/8 | Rest values | whole, 1/2, 1/4 |

Example: a) Rhythm

Example: b) Violin Passage

# Aural Tests

The candidate will be required:

i)  to clap back the rhythmic pattern of a short melody in 2/4, 3/4 or 4/4 time, consisting of whole, half, dotted half, quarter, dotted quarter and eighth notes, after it has been played twice by the Examiner at the keyboard. Following is the approximate level of difficulty:

ii) to identify *major* or *minor* triad chords played once by the Examer in solid form and in close, root position.

iii) to identify *major* or *harmonic minor* or *melodic minor* scales played once by the Examiner, ascending and descending, at a moderate tempo.

iv) the *major* or *minor* common [four-note] chord of any key will be played once by the Examiner in broken form slowly, ascending and descending. The chord will be in root position. One of the four notes will then be re-sounded for the candidate to identify, by saying, at the candidate's choice:

      EITHER      (1) its interval number [1, 3, 5, 8]
      OR          (2) its tonic sol-fa name [doh, me, sol, upper doh]

# Viva Voce

Candidates must be prepared to give verbal answers to questions on the TWO List pieces selected for the examination. Candidates must ensure that all teaching notes and other written comments are removed from the score before the examination. The questions will include the following elements:

i)  to find and explain all of the signs (including clefs, time signatures, key signatures, accidentals, etc.), articulation markings (legato, staccato, accents, phrase or slur markings, etc.), dynamic and tempo markings, and other musical terms as they may be found in the two selected pieces.

ii) without reference to the score, to give the title, key and composer of the piece.

iii) to explain the meaning of the title of the piece

# GRADE FOUR

Length of the examination: 25 minutes

Examination Fee: Please consult the current examination application form for the schedule of fees.

Co-requisite: None. There is NO written examination co-requisite for the awarding of the Grade 4 Practical Certificate.

## Requirements & Marking

| Requirement | Total Marks |
|---|---|
| TWO LIST PIECES | |
| One from each of | |
| List A | 16 |
| List B | 16 |
| TWO STUDIES | |
| One from Study List A (Baroque/Classical) | 6 |
| One from Study List B (Romantic/20th Century) | 6 |
| ONE SUPPLEMENTARY PIECE | 8 |
| TECHNICAL TESTS | |
| Scales & Arpeggios | 16 |
| SIGHT READING | |
| Rhythm Pattern | 3 |
| Playing | 7 |
| AURAL TESTS | 10 |
| VIVA VOCE | 8 |
| MARKS FOR MEMORY | |
| List pieces only (2 marks each) | 4 |
| TOTAL POSSIBLE MARKS | 100 |

*NOTE: The examination program must include at least ONE work by a Canadian composer. The Canadian work may be chosen from the List Pieces OR as the Supplementary Piece. Candidates who fail to include a Canadian work will be subject to an automatic deduction from their over-all total mark.*

## Pieces

Candidates must be prepared to play TWO pieces from the list below, chosen to contrast in style, key, tempo, etc. Your choice must include TWO different composers. All pieces requiring accompaniment must be played with accompaniment. All pieces were available in print at the time the syllabus was prepared. Although suggested editions have been given below to assist candidates in identifying and purchasing music, ANY STANDARD EDITION may be used for the examination.

   * = Canadian composer

## LIST A

**ALBINONI, T.**
Allegro (*Sonata, Op. VI, No. 7*) — Presser
(*Baroque Music for Violin*)
**BACH, J. S.**
Gavotte in D (*Suzuki Violin School, Vol. 3*) — Summy Birchard
Musette in D (arr. Seely-Brown) — Fischer
(*10 Little Classics for Violin*)
Bourées in G and G minor BWV 1009 — Summy Birchard
(*Suzuki Violin School, Vol. 3*)
**CORRETTE, M.**
Coucou (*Music for Violin & Piano II*) — Schott
Allegro in D minor (*Music for Violin & Piano II*) — Schott
**DANCLA, C.**
Air with Variations Op. 123, No. 7 — Harris
**HUBER, A.**
Student's Concertino Op. 8, No. 4 (*Fun with Solos*) — CMS
**KUCHLER, F.**
Concertino in D, Op. 12 (*Violin Series 4*) — Harris
Choose ANY TWO contrasting movements
**LECLAIR, J. M.**
Musette (*An Evening of Violin Classics*) — Schirmer
**MARTINU, B.**
Sonatina — Malantrich (Prague)
**RIEDING, O.**
Concerto in D, Op. 36 — Bosworth
Choose ANY TWO contrasting movements
Concerto in B minor, Op. 35 — Bosworth
Choose ANY TWO contrasting movements
Rondo, Op. 22, No. 3 — Bosworth
**VIVALDI, A.**
Gavotte, Op. 11, No. 11 (*Baroque Music for Violin*) — Presser
**WOELBER, F.**
Student's Concerto in D — Fischer

## LIST B

**\*ADASKIN, M.**
Gretchen at Seven — CMC
**\*BECKWITH, J.**
Sheep (*Eight Miniatures*) — Harris
**BIRKENSTOCK, J.**
Sarabande, Op. 1, No. 5 (*Baroque Music for Violin*) — Presser
**\*BOUCHARD, RÉMI**
String Along (*Violin Series 4*) — Harris
**BRAHMS, J.**
Hungarian Dance in G minor, No. 5 — Universal
(*Universal Geigen Album 3*)
**CHOPIN, F.**
Mazurka, Op. 7, No. 2 (*Universal Geigen Album 1*) — Universal

**\*COULTHARD, J.**
A Song for Bedtime (*Encore Series, Book II*) — Harris
Let's Play (*Encore Series, Book II*) — Harris
**DVORAK, A.**
Waltz in A, Op. 54, No. 1 (*Universal Geigen Album 1*) — Universal
**\*ETHRIDGE, J.**
"Wrong Note" Caprice (*Encore Series, Book II*) — Harris
**GREEN**
Playful Rondo — Fischer
**HANDEL, G. F.**
Air from "Water Music" (*Universal Geigen Album 1*) — Universal
**HAYDN, F. J.**
Serenade from String Quartet Op. 3, No. 5 — Schirmer
(*An Evening of Violin Classics*)
**\*HYSLOP, R.**
Awesome Opossum (*Music Stands*) — Harris
Canzonetta (*String Knots*) — Harris
Droll Troll (*Music Stands*) — Harris
Firecrackers Bang Bang (*Music Stands*) — Harris
Sliding Around (*Music Stands*) — Harris
**KABALEVSKY, D.**
*20 Pieces for Violin and Piano, Op. 80* — Leeds (Can.)
Choose ANY ONE of
No. 15 On Holiday
No. 16 Summer Song
**KOHLER, O.**
Gypsy Melody, Op. 160, No. 3 — Schirmer
(*An Evening of Violin Classics*)
**\*KYMLICKA, M.**
Allegro (*Simple Music for Violin and Piano*) — CMC
Tempo di Menuetto (*Simple Music for Violin and Piano*) — CMC
**LEWANDO**
Minuet in the Old Style — Bosworth
**MARTINI, J. P. E.**
Andantino (*An Evening of Violin Classics*) — Schirmer
**NELSON, S.**
Skye Boat Song (*Moving Up Again*) — Boosey & Hawkes
**PARASHKEV, H.**
Rondino in A (*The Young Violinist's Repertoire Book IV*) — Faber
**SCHUBERT, F.**
Entr'acte Music from "Rosamunde" — Universal
(*Universal Geigen Album I*)
German Dance (*The Young Violinist's Repertoire Book IV*) — Faber
Heidenroslein (*Universal Geigen Album I*) — Universal
**SCHUMANN, R.**
Traümerei (*Universal Geigen Album I*) — Universal
**SMETANA, B.**
Lullaby from "The Kiss" (*Universal Geigen Album I*) — Universal
**TCHAIKOVSKY, P. I.**
Chanson Triste (*Douze Morceux, Op. 40*) — Faber
(*The Young Violinist's Repertoire Book IV*)
March of the Tin Soldiers (*An Evening of Violin Classics*) Schirmer

# Studies

Candidates must be prepared to play TWO contrasting studies in different keys, ONE from Study List A and ONE from Study List B, below. Memorization is recommended, although not required.

| STUDY LIST A | STUDY LIST B |
|---|---|

**KAYSER, H. E.**
*Elem. & Progressive Studies for Violin, Op. 20, Book 1*   Schirmer
Choose ANY ONE of
Nos. 4, 5, 8

**WOHLFAHRT, F.**
*Fifty Easy Melodious Studies for Violin, Op. 74, Book 1*   Schirmer
Choose ANY ONE of
Nos. 18, 21, 25

**SITT, H.**
*Studies for Violin, Op. 32, Book 2*   Carl Fischer
Choose ANY ONE of
Nos. 21-24

**WOHLFAHRT, F.**
*Sixty Studies for Violin, Op. 45, Book 2*   Schirmer
Choose ANY ONE of
Nos. 36, 39

## Supplementary Piece

Candidates must be prepared to play ONE Supplementary Piece. This piece need not be from the Syllabus lists, and may be chosen entirely at the discretion of the teacher and student. It may represent a period or style of piece not already included in the examination program, but which holds special interest for the candidate. The choice must be within the following guidelines:

1) The equivalent level of difficulty of the piece may be at a higher grade level, providing it is within the technical and musical grasp of the candidate.

2) Pieces below the equivalent of Grade 3 level are not acceptable.

3) The piece must be for solo violin (with or without piano accompaniment). Duets and trios are not acceptable.

4) Candidates with exceptional talent for improvisation may wish to improvise on a theme of their choice. In this case, items 1 and 2 (above) will apply. Marks will be given for originality, musical inventiveness, and structural unity.

Special approval is not required for the Supplementary Piece. However, poor suitability of the choice may be reflected in the mark. Memorization is encouraged, although NOT required.

## Technical Tests

All technical tests must be played from memory, evenly, with good tone, secure intonation, with all of the listed bowings, ascending and descending, in the keys stated.

### SCALES

*ALL scales to be played from memory, ascending AND descending.*

| | Keys | Octaves | Note Values | M.M. $\boldsymbol{\downarrow}$= | Bowings |
|---|---|---|---|---|---|
| Major | C, D, E | 2 | ♪ | 72 | ♪♪♪♪ |
| Harmonic Minor | c, d | 2 | ♪ | 72 | ♪♪♪♪ |
| Melodic Minor | c, d | 2 | ♪ | 72 | ♪♪♪♪ |
| Chromatic | A♭ | 1 | ♩ | 84 | detaché |
| Broken Intervals in 3ʳᵈˢ | C | 1 | ♩ | 72 | ♩ ♩ (see example below) |

Example: Broken (Running) 3rds

15

## ARPEGGIOS

*ALL arpeggios to be played from memory, ascending AND descending.  Do NOT repeat the top note.*

| | Keys | Octaves | Note Values | M.M. | Bowings |
|---|---|---|---|---|---|
| Major | C, **D**, E | 2 | ♩ | 72 | |
| Minor | c, d | 2 | ♩ | 72 | |
| Dominant 7ths | In the key of C | 2 | ♩ | 72 | detaché |

# Sight Reading

Candidates are required to perform at sight a) a rhythmic exercise and b) a passage of violin score as described below. The candidate will be given a brief period to scan the score, but not to "practise silently" before beginning to play. Candidates must perform each section without counting aloud. It is recommended that candidates maintain a steady beat, and avoid the unnecessary repetition caused by attempting to correct errors during the performance.

| *a) Rhythm* | *b) Violin Passage* |
|---|---|
| To tap or play on one note (at the candidate's choice) a simple rhythm. | To play at sight a simple melody, within the range of $G_1$-$G^1$, treble clef |
| Length       4 bars | Keys       C, G, D, A, F Major & A, E minor |
| Time signature       2/4, 3/4, 4/4 | Length       4-8 bars |
| Note values       whole, 1/2, dotted 1/2, 1/4, 1/8, dotted 1/4 followed by 1/8, & dotted 1/8 followed by 1/16 | Time signature       2/4, 3/4, 4/4 |
| | Note values       whole, dotted 1/2, 1/2, 1/4, 1/8 |
| Rest values       whole, 1/2, 1/4, 1/8 | Rest values       whole, 1/2, 1/4 |

Example: a) Rhythm

Example: b) Violin Passage

# Aural Tests

The candidate will be required:

i)    at the candidate's choice, to play back OR sing back to any vowel, a short melody of six to eight notes, based on the first five notes of a major scale, after the Examiner has:

     ✓ named the key [only the major keys of *C, F, G* or *D* will be used]

     ✓ played the 4-note chord on the tonic [broken form]

     ✓ played the melody twice.

The melody will begin on the tonic note. Following is the approximate level of difficulty:

ii) to identify any of the following intervals after each one has been played once by the Examiner in broken form:

| **ABOVE a given note** | **BELOW a note** |
| --- | --- |
| *major 3rd* | *perfect 4th* |
| *minor 3rd* | *perfect 5th* |
| *perfect 4th* | *perfect octave* |
| *perfect 5th* | |
| *perfect octave* | |

iii) to identify *major* or *minor* triad chords, solid form, in close, root position only. Each triad chord will be played ONCE by the examiner.

iv) to state whether a short piece in *chorale* style, about 6 to 8 in length, is in a *major* or a *minor* key, and whether the final cadence is either **Perfect** (V-I) or **Interrupted/Deceptive** (V-VI).

# Viva Voce

Candidates must be prepared to give verbal answers to questions on the TWO List pieces selected for the examination. Candidates must ensure that all teaching notes and other written comments are removed from the score before the examination. The questions will include the following elements:

i) to find and explain all of the signs (including clefs, time signatures, key signatures, accidentals, etc.), articulation markings (legato, staccato, accents, phrase or slur markings, etc.), dynamic and tempo markings, and other musical terms and signs as they may be found in the two selected pieces.

ii) without reference to the score, to give the title, key and composer of the piece.

iii) to explain the meaning of the title of the piece.

iv) to give a few relevant details about the composer.

v) with direct reference to the score, to explain briefly simple form and key structures, including any obvious modulations.

# GRADE FIVE

Length of the examination:     25 minutes

Examination Fee:               Please consult the current examination application form for the schedule of fees.

Co-requisite:                  Successful completion of the following written examination is required for the awarding of the Grade 5 Practical Certificate.
                               ***THEORY 1***

## Requirements & Marking

| Requirement | Total Marks |
|---|---|
| TWO LIST PIECES | |
| One from each of | |
|    List A (Baroque/Classical) | 17 |
|    List B (Romantic/20th Century) | 17 |
| TWO STUDIES | |
|    One from Study List A | 6 |
|    One from Study List B | 6 |
| ONE SUPPLEMENTARY PIECE | 8 |
| TECHNICAL TESTS | |
|    Scales & Arpeggios | 16 |
| SIGHT READING | |
|    Rhythm Pattern | 3 |
|    Playing | 7 |
| AURAL TESTS | 8 |
| VIVA VOCE | 8 |
| MARKS FOR MEMORY | |
| List pieces only (2 marks each) | 4 |
| TOTAL POSSIBLE MARKS | 100 |

*NOTE: The examination program must include at least ONE work by a Canadian composer. The Canadian work may be chosen from the List Pieces OR as the Supplementary Piece. Candidates who fail to include a Canadian work will be subject to an automatic deduction from their over-all total mark.*

## Pieces

Candidates must be prepared to play TWO pieces from the list below, chosen to contrast in style, key, tempo, etc. Your choice must include TWO different composers. All pieces requiring accompaniment must be played with accompaniment. All pieces were available in print at the time the syllabus was prepared. Although suggested editions have been given below to assist candidates in identifying and purchasing music, ANY STANDARD EDITION may be used for the examination.

\* = *Canadian composer*

## LIST A

**BACH, J. S.**
Gavotte in D (*Cello Suite No. 6, BWV 1012*)    Summy Birchard
(*Suzuki Violin School, Vol. 5*)
Gavotte in D (arr. Saenger)    Fischer
*10 Little Classics for Violin (arr. Seely-Brown)*    Fischer
Choose ANY ONE of
Giguetta in C
Sarabanda in C (No. 5)
Sarabanda in C (No. 6)

**BOCCHERINI, L.**
(Celebrated) Minuet from Quintet in E    Any edition

**DEBOISMORTIER, J. B. (ED. DOFLEIN)**
Allegretto (*Music for Violin & Piano I*)    Schott

**CORELLI, A.**
Allemande, Op. 5, No. 10 (*Baroque Music for Violin*)    Presser

**HÄNDEL, G. F.**
Gigue from Concerto Grosso No. 9    Schirmer
(*Masterworks for the Young Violinist*)

**HAYDN, F. J.**
Minuetto from *Symphony No. 14*    Kendor

**MOZART, W. A.**
Aria in G (*The Young Violinist's Repertoire Book 4*)    Faber

**PURCELL, H.**
Allegro and Andante Cantabile    Lengnick

**SEITZ, F.**
Student's Concerto, Op. 13, No. 2 (1st mov't only)    CMS
(*Fun With Solos*)
Concerto No. 2 (3rd mov't only)    Summy Birchard
(*Suzuki Violin School, Vol. 4*)
Concerto No. 5 (*Suzuki Violin School, Vol. 4*)    Summy Birchard
Choose EITHER 1st mov't OR 3rd mov't

**STEIBELT, D. (ED. DOFLEIN)**
Allegro Moderato & Rondo (*Sonatine Op. 33, No. 1*)    Schott
(*Music for Violin & Piano II*)

**VERACINI, F. M.**
Largo e Cantabile, Op. 11, No. 7    Presser
(*Baroque Music for Violin*)

## LIST B

**\*ADASKIN, M.**
Dedication    CMC
Quiet Song    Leeds

**BOHM, C.**
Sarabande (*Fun with Solos*)    CMS

**\*COULTHARD, J.**
A Quiet Afternoon    CMC
On the March    Berandol

**\*DOLIN, S.**
Little Sombrero    Berandol
2 x 3    Harris

**\*DUKE, D.**
Chaconne (*Encore Series Book V*)    Harris

**ELLERTON, G.**
Gavotte, Op. 21, No. 3 (*6 Morceau Mignons*)    Bosworth

**\*FIALA, G.**
Wallaby's Lullaby    CMC

**\*FLEMING, R.**
Yukon Tune    CMC

**\*HYSLOP, R.**
Ballade (*String Knots*)    Harris
Chants D'Inuit (*Bow Ties*)    Harris
Coastin' (*Bow Ties*)    Harris
España (*String Knots*)    Harris
The River (*Bow Ties*)    Harris

**\*JAQUE, R.**
Daussila    Berandol/BMI

**KABALEVSKY, D.**
*20 Pieces for Violin and Piano*    Leeds (Can.)
Choose ANY ONE of
No. 17 The Procession
No. 18 Ping Pong

**\*KENINS, T.**
Recitative and Duet    CMC

**MOLLENHAUER, E.**
The Infant Paganini    Fischer

**NELSON, S.**
Caprice (*Moving Up Again*)    Boosey & Hawkes

**PORTNOFF, L.**
*Russian Fantasias*    Bosworth
Choose ANY ONE of
Nos. 1, 4

**SCHUBERT, F.**
Moment Musical (*Universal Geigen Album I*)    Universal

**SMETANA, B.**
Furiante (*The Bartered Bride*)    Universal
(*Universal Geigen Album II*)

**TCHAIKOVSKY, P.I.**
Mazurka (*Piano Trio, Op. 50*)    Schirmer
(*Masterworks for the Young Violinist*)
Waltz of the Flowers    Universal
(*Universal Geigen Album II*)

**TRADITIONAL**
Hebrew Prayer (*The Young Violinist's Repertoire Book 4*)    Faber

**WAGNER, R.**
Prize Song (*Die Meistersinger*)    Universal
(*Universal Geigen Album I*)

**WARNER, H. E.**
Perpetuum Mobile, Op. 60, No. 3    Lengnick

**WEISS, J.**
The Red Sarafan (Russian Folk Song), Op. 38, No. 40    Schirmer
(*An Evening of Violin Classics*)

# Studies

Candidates must be prepared to play TWO contrasting studies in different keys, ONE from Study List A and ONE from Study List B, below. Memorization is recommended, although not required.

### STUDY LIST A

**TROTT, J.**
*Melodious Double Stops, Book 1*    Schirmer
Choose ANY ONE of
Nos. 1, 2, 3, 4, 5, 6, 7, 8, 9

### STUDY LIST B

**SITT, H.**
*Studies for Violin, Op. 32, Book 2*    Carl Fischer
Choose ANY ONE of
Nos. 26, 27, 28
(continued on next page)

**STUDY LIST B (CONT'D.)**

**WOHLFAHRT, F.**
*Sixty Studies for Violin, Op. 45, Book 2*   Schirmer
Choose ANY ONE of
Nos. 41, 42

**WOHLFAHRT, F.**
*Fifty Easy Melodious Studies for Violin, Op. 74, Bk 2*   Schirmer
Choose ANY ONE of
Nos. 27, 28, 29, 30

## Supplementary Piece

Candidates must be prepared to play ONE Supplementary Piece. This piece need not be from the Syllabus lists, and may be chosen entirely at the discretion of the teacher and student. It may represent a period or style of piece not already included in the examination program, but which holds special interest for the candidate. The choice must be within the following guidelines:

1) The equivalent level of difficulty of the piece may be at a higher grade level, providing it is within the technical and musical grasp of the candidate.

2) Pieces below the equivalent of Grade 4 level are not acceptable.

3) The piece must be for solo violin (with or without piano accompaniment). Duets and trios are not acceptable.

4) Candidates with exceptional talent for improvisation may wish to improvise on a theme of their choice. In this case, items 1 and 2 (above) will apply. Marks will be given for originality, musical inventiveness, and structural unity.

Special approval is not required for the Supplementary Piece. However, poor suitability of the choice may be reflected in the mark. Memorization is encouraged, although NOT required.

## Technical Tests

All technical tests must be played from memory, evenly, with good tone, secure intonation, with all of the listed bowings, ascending and descending, in the keys noted.

### SCALES

*ALL scales to be played from memory, ascending AND descending.*

| | Keys | Octaves | Note Values | M.M. ♩= | Bowings |
|---|---|---|---|---|---|
| Major | E♭, F | 2 | ♪ | 80 | |
| | G | 3 | ♪ | 80 | |
| Harmonic Minor | e♭, f | 2 | ♪ | 80 | |
| Melodic Minor | e♭, f | 2 | ♪ | 80 | |
| Chromatic | G, A | 2 | ♪ | 80 | detaché |
| Broken Intervals/ Double Stops in 3rds | G, A | 1 | ♩ | 80 | |
| Broken Intervals/ Double Stops in 6ths | G, A | 1 | ♩ | 80 | |
| Broken Intervals/ Double Stops in 8ves | G, A | 1 | ♩ | 80 | |

Example: a) Broken Intervals / Double Stops

**ARPEGGIOS**

*ALL arpeggios to be played from memory, ascending AND descending. Do NOT repeat the top note.*

| | Keys | Octaves | Note Values | M.M. | Bowings |
|---|---|---|---|---|---|
| Major | E♭, F, G | 2 3 | ♫♫ *3* | 60 | *3* ♫♫ |
| Minor | e♭, f | 2 | ♫♫ *3* | 60 | *3* ♫♫ |
| Dominant 7ths | In the keys of **D, E** | 2 | ♩ | 60 | ♩ ♩ |
| Diminished 7ths | In the key of a | 1 | ♩ | 60 | detaché |

# Sight Reading

Candidates are required to perform at sight a) a rhythmic exercies and b) a passage of violin score as described below. The candidate will be given a brief period to scan the score, but not to "practise silently" before beginning to play. Candidates must perform each section without counting aloud. It is recommended that candidates maintain a steady beat, and avoid the unnecessary repetition caused by attempting to correct errors during the performance.

| *a) Rhythm* | | *b) Violin Passage* | |
|---|---|---|---|
| To tap, clap or play on one note (at the candidate's choice) a simple rhythm | | To play at sight a simple melody, about equal in difficulty to pieces of Grade 3 level. | |
| Length | 4 bars | Keys | C, G, D, A, F, B♭ Major & |
| Time signature | 2/4, 3/4, 4/4 | | a, e, d minor |
| Note values | variety of values including triplets and ties | Length | 8-12 bars |
| Rest values | whole, 1/2, 1/4, 1/8 | | |

Example: a) Rhythm

Example: b) Violin Passage

# Aural Tests

The candidate will be required:

i) at the candidate's choice, to play back OR sing back to any vowel a short melody of six to eight notes, in 2/4, 3/4, or 4/4 time, based on the first five notes and the lower leading tone of a *major* scale, after the Examiner has:
   ✓ named the key [C, F, G or D major]
   ✓ played the 4-note chord on the tonic [broken form]
   ✓ played the melody twice.

The melody will begin on the tonic note. Following is the approximate level of difficulty:

ii) to identify any of the following intervals after each one has been played once by the Examiner in broken form:

**ABOVE a note**
*major 3rd*
*minor 3rd*
*perfect 4th*
*perfect 5th*
*major 6th*
*minor 6th*
*perfect octave*

**BELOW a note**
*major 3rd*
*minor 3rd*
*perfect 4th*
*perfect 5th*
*perfect octave*

iii) to identify *major* or *minor* triads and *dominant 7th* chords, solid form, in close, root position only. Each triad/chord will be played ONCE by the Examiner.

iv) to state whether a short piece in *chorale* style is in a *major* or a *minor* key, and whether the final cadence is **Perfect** (V-I) or **Plagal** (IV-I).

## Viva Voce

Candidates must be prepared to give verbal answers on the TWO List pieces selected for the examination. Candidates must ensure that all teaching notes and other written comments are removed from the score before the examination. The questions will include the following elements:

i) to find and explain all of the signs (including clefs, time signatures, key signatures, accidentals, etc.), articulation markings (legato, staccato, accents, phrase or slur markings, etc.), dynamic and tempo markings, and other musical terms as they may be found in the two selected pieces.

ii) without reference to the score, to give the title, key and composer of the piece.

iii) to explain the meaning of the title of the piece.

iv) to give a few relevant details about the composer.

v) with direct reference to the score, to explain briefly simple form and key structures, including any obvious modulations.

---

# GRADE SIX

Length of the examination:     30 minutes

Examination Fee:     Please consult the current examination application form for the schedule of fees.

Co-requisite:     Successful completion of the following written examination is required for the awarding of the Grade 6 Practical Certificate.
**THEORY 2**

## Requirements & Marking

| Requirement | Total Marks |
|---|---|
| THREE LIST PIECES | |
| One from each of | |
|    List A (Concerto) | 13 |
|    List B (Sonata) | 12 |
|    List C (Piece) | 11 |
| TWO STUDIES | |
|    ONE from Study List A | 6 |
|    ONE from Study List B | 6 |
| ONE SUPPLEMENTARY PIECE | 8 |
| TECHNICAL TESTS | |
|    Scales & Arpeggios | 16 |
| SIGHT READING | |
|    Rhythm Pattern | 3 |
|    Playing | 7 |
| AURAL TESTS | 8 |
| VIVA VOCE | 6 |
| MARKS FOR MEMORY | |
| List A and List C pieces only (2 marks each) | 4 |
| TOTAL POSSIBLE MARKS | 100 |

*NOTE: The examination program must include at least ONE work by a Canadian composer. The Canadian work may be chosen from the List Pieces OR as the Supplementary Piece. Candidates who fail to include a Canadian work will be subject to an automatic deduction from their over-all total mark.*

## Pieces

Candidates must be prepared to play TWO pieces from the list below, chosen to contrast in style, key, tempo, etc. Your choice must include TWO different composers. All pieces requiring accompaniment must be played with accompaniment. All pieces were available in print at the time the syllabus was prepared. Although suggested editions have been given below to assist candidates in identifying and purchasing music, ANY STANDARD EDITION may be used for the examination.

    * = *Canadian composer*

## LIST A

**HUBER, A.**
Student Concertino in G, Op. 6, No. 2 (complete)    Any edition
**PERLMAN, G.**
Israeli Concertino    Boosey & Hawkes
Choose ANY ONE movement
**RIEDING, O.**
Concerto in A minor, Op. 21 (1st mov't)    Boswell
**SEITZ, F.**
Concerto in G minor, Op. 12, No. 3 (1st mov't)    Any edition
**VIVALDI, A.**
Concerto in A minor, Op. 3, No. 6    Any edition
Choose EITHER 1st movement OR 3rd movement
Concerto in G, Op. 3, No. 3 (1st mov't)

## LIST B

**BACH, J. C.**
Sonata in G (*Sonatas by Old Masters*)    Universal
**HANDEL, G. F.**
Sonata No. 3 in F (Suzuki Violin School, Vol. 6)    Summy Birchard
Choose ANY TWO contrasting movements
**HASLINGER, T.**
Two Sonatinas, Op. 12    Editio Musica Budapest
(*Easy Classical Sonatas*)
Choose EITHER Sonatina I OR Sonatina II (complete)
**HAYDN, F. J.**
Sonata in G, Hob. XVI:43bis. (complete)    Editio Musica Budapest
(*Easy Classical Sonatas*)
**LECLAIR, J. M.**
Sonata in E minor (*Sonatas by Old Masters*)    Universal
Choose ANY TWO contrasting movements
**MATTHESON, J.**
Sonata in E minor (complete) (*Sonatas by Old Masters*)    Universal
**TARTINI, G.**
Sonata in B flat (*Sonatas by Old Masters*)    Universal
Allegro AND Largo
**VERACINI, F. M.**
Gigue from Sonata in D minor    Summy Birchard
(*Suzuki Violin School, Vol. 5*)
Sonata, Op. 1, No. 1 in G minor    Associated Music Publishers
(*3 Sonatas for Violin and Piano*)
Choose ANY TWO contrasting movements
**WANHAL, J. B.**
Three Sonatas (*Easy Classical Sonatas*)    Edition Musica Budapest
Choose ANY TWO (Complete) of
Sonata I
Sonata II
Sonata III

## LIST C

**ALBINONI, T.**
Allegro from *Sonata Op. VI, No. 7*    Presser
(*Baroque Music for Violin*)
**BACH, J. S.**
Gigue (*Suzuki Violin School, Vol. 6*)    Summy Birchard
**BACH, J. S./GOUNOD, C. (ARR. AMBROSIO)**
Ave Maria/Meditation on the First Prelude    Fischer
**BIRKENSTOCK, J. A.**
Siciliano, Op. 1, No. 5 (*Baroque Music for Violin*)    Presser

**BOHM, C.**
Spanish Dance    Lengnick
**BRAHMS, J.**
Wiegenlied, Op. 49, No. 4    Schirmer
(*All Time Favorite Violin Solos*)
**CORELLI, A.**
Courante in F (*Suzuki Violin School, Vol. 6*)    Summy Birchard
Corrente in F, Op. 5, No. 7 (*Baroque Music for Violin*)    Presser
Introduzione and Giga da Camara (arr. Moffat)    Any Edition
**\*COULTHARD, J.**
Little French Suite (*Encore Series 6*)    Harris
Choose ANY TWO contrasting movements
**DANCLA, C.**
*Air Variés, Op. 89*    Any edition
Choose ANY ONE of
Nos. IV, V, VI
**DEBERIOT, C. (ARR. BARBER)**
Air Varié    Praeludio
**DEBUSSY, C.**
La fille aux cheveux de lin (*Universal Geigen Album III*)    Universal
**ELMAN, M.**
Canto Amoroso    Schott
**\*ETHRIDGE, J.**
Elegy (*Encore Series 6*)    Harris
Fairy Tale (*Encore Series 6*)    Harris
**GRIEG, E.**
Waltz (*Lyric Pieces, Op. 12*) (*Solos for the Violin Player*)    Schirmer
**\*HYSLOP, R.**
Copycat    CMC
Les Gars de Chicoutimi (*Bow Ties*)    Harris
Sausilito (*Bow Ties*)    Harris
Will o' Wisp    CMC
**\*KYMLICKA, M.**
Andante (*Simple Music for Violin & Piano, Book 1*)    CMC
Allegretto (*Simple Music for Violin & Piano, Book 1*)    CMC
**MENDELSSOHN, L.**
Mosquito Dance (*L. Mendelssohn Miniatures*)    Bosworth
**MOZART, W. A. (ARR. BURMESTER)**
Menuet in D (*Selected Pieces of Old Masters*)    Harris
**NELSON, S.**
Motu Perpetuo (*Moving Up Again*)    Boosey & Hawkes
**\*PEPA, M.**
Danses Concertantes #1    CMC
**\*POLSON, A.**
A Dream (*Violin Series 6*)    Harris
**RAMEAU, J. P.**
Gavotte in D (*Suzuki Violin School, Vol. 6*)    Summy Birchard
**REBEL, J. F.**
The Bells (*Solos for the Violin Player*)    Schirmer
**SENAILLÉ, J. B.**
Allegro Spiritoso (*Solos for the Violin Player*)    Schirmer
**SCHUBERT, F. (ARR. SITT)**
Serenade "Leise flehen meine Lieder"    Schirmer
(*All Time Favorite Violin Solos*)
**SHOSTAKOVICH, D.**
Dance (*Violin Series 5*)    Harris
**SMITH, L.**
Tambourin (*Violin Series 5*)    Harris
**WAGNER, R.**
O Star of Eve from "Tannhauser"    Universal
(*Universal Geigen Album III*)
**VON WEBER, C. M.**
Country Dance (*Suzuki Violin School, Vol. 5*)    Summy Birchard

# Studies

Candidates must be prepared to play TWO contrasting studies in different keys, ONE from Study List A and ONE from Study List B, below. Memorization is recommended, although not required.

| STUDY LIST A | | STUDY LIST B | |
|---|---|---|---|
| **TROTT, J.** | | **MAZAS** | |
| *Melodious Double Stops, Book 1* | Schirmer | *75 Melodious & Progressive Studies, Op. 36, Book 1* | Schirmer |
| Nos. 13, 14, 15, 16, 17, 18, 19, 20 | | Nos. 2, 3, 5, 6 | |
| | | **WOHLFAHRT, F.** | |
| | | *Sixty Studies for Violin, Op. 45, Book 2* | Schirmer |
| | | Nos. 50, 51, 52, 53, 54, 55 | |

# Supplementary Piece

Candidates must be prepared to play ONE Supplementary Piece. This piece need not be from the Syllabus lists, and may be chosen entirely at the discretion of the teacher and student. It may represent a period or style of piece not already included in the examination program, but which holds special interest for the candidate. The choice must be within the following guidelines:

1)  The equivalent level of difficulty of the piece may be at a higher grade level, providing it is within the technical and musical grasp of the candidate.

2)  Pieces below the equivalent of Grade 5 level are not acceptable.

3)  The piece must be for solo violin (with or without piano accompaniment). Duets and trios are not acceptable.

4)  Candidates with exceptional talent for improvisation may wish to improvise on a theme of their choice. In this case, items 1 and 2 (above) will apply. Marks will be given for originality, musical inventiveness, and structural unity.

Special approval is not required for the Supplementary Piece. However, poor suitability of the choice may be reflected in the mark. Memorization is encouraged, although NOT required.

# Technical Tests

*All technical tests must be played from memory, evenly, with good tone, secure intonation, with all of the listed bowing, ascending and descending.*

## SCALES
*ALL scales to be played from memory, ascending AND descending.*

| | Keys | Octaves | Note Values | M.M. $\quad=$ | Bowings |
|---|---|---|---|---|---|
| Major | A♭, A, B♭ | 3 | ♪ | 84 | |
| Harmonic Minor | a♭, a, b♭ | 3 | ♪ | 84 | |
| Melodic Minor | a♭, a, b♭ | 3 | ♪ | 84 | |
| Chromatic | B♭, B | 2 | ♪ | 84 | |
| Broken Intervals/ Double Stops in 3rds | A♭, B♭ | 1 | ♩ | 72 | |
| Broken Intervals/ Double Stops in 6ths | A♭, B♭ | 1 | ♩ | 72 | |
| Broken Intervals/ Double Stops in 8ves | A♭, B♭ | 1 | ♩ | 72 | |

*(see page 20 for examples of broken intervals/double stops)*

**ARPEGGIOS**

*ALL arpeggios to be played from memory, ascending AND descending. Do NOT repeat the top note.*

| | Keys | Octaves | Note Values | M.M. | Bowings Comments |
|---|---|---|---|---|---|
| Major | Ab, A, Bb | 3 | ♫♫ *3* | 72 | *3* *3* |
| Minor | ab, a, bb | 3 | ♫♫ *3* | 72 | *3* *3* |
| Dominant 7ths | In the keys of D, E | 2 | ♪ | 72 | |
| Diminished 7ths | In the keys of d, e | 1 | ♪ | 72 | |

## Sight Reading

Candidates are required to perform at sight a) a rhythmic exercise and b) a passage of violin score as described below. The candidate will be given a brief period to scan the score, but not to "practise silently" before beginning to play. Candidates must perform each section without counting aloud. It is recommended that candidates maintain a steady beat, and avoid the unnecessary repetition caused by attempting to correct errors during the performance.

| *a) Rhythm* | *b) Violin Passage* |
|---|---|
| To tap, clap or play on one note (at the candidate's choice) a simple rhythm | To play at sight a simple melody, about equal in difficulty to pieces of Grade 4 level. |
| Length 4 bars | Keys Major & Minor up to and including |
| Time signature 3/4, 4/4 | 3 sharps or flats |
| Note values variety of values including | Length 8-16 bars |
| triplets and ties | |
| Rest values whole, 1/2, 1/4, 1/8 | |

Example: a) Rhythm

## Aural Tests

The candidate will be required:

i) at the candidate's choice, to play back OR sing back to any vowel a short melody of six to eight notes, in 2/4, 3/4 or 4/4 time, based on the first five notes and the lower leading tone in a *major* or *minor* key, after the Examiner has:
   ✓ named the key [up to and including two sharps or flats]
   ✓ played the 4-note chord on the tonic in broken form
   ✓ played the melody twice.

The melody will begin on the tonic note. Following is the approximate level of difficulty:

ii)  to identify any of the following intervals after the Examiner has played each one once in broken form:

**ABOVE a note**
*major and minor 2nd*
*major and minor 3rd*
*perfect 4th*
*perfect 5th*
*major and minor 6th*
*perfect octave*

**BELOW a note**
*major and minor 3rd*
*perfect 4th*
*perfect 5th*
*minor 6th*
*perfect octave*

iii)  to identify any of the following triads/chords when played once by the Examiner in solid form, in close, root position:
   *major* and *minor* triads (3-note)
   *dominant 7th* chords (4-note)
   *diminished 7th* chords (4-note)

iv)  to state whether a short piece in *chorale* style is in a *major* or a *minor* key, and whether the final cadence is **Perfect** (V-I), **Plagal** (IV-I), or **Interrupted/Deceptive** (V-VI).

# Viva Voce

Candidates must be prepared to give verbal answers to questions on the THREE list pieces selected for the examination. Candidates must ensure that all teaching notes and other written comments are removed from the score before the examination. The questions will include the following elements:

i)  to find and explain all of the signs (including clefs, time signatures, key signatures, accidentals, etc.), articulation markings (legato, staccato, accents, phrase or slur markings, etc.), dynamic and tempo markings, and other musical terms as they may be found in the three selected pieces.

ii)  without reference to the score, to give the title, key and composer of the piece.

iii)  to explain the meaning of the title of the piece.

iv)  to give a few relevant details about the composer.

v)  with direct reference to the score, to explain briefly the form of the piece (for example, binary or ternary form, dance piece, sonata, etc.)

vi)  with direct reference to the score, to explain briefly the key structure, including any modulations.

---

# GRADE SEVEN

Length of the examination: 30 minutes

Examination Fee: Please consult the current examination application form for the schedule of fees.

Co-requisite: Successful completion of the following written examination is required for the awarding of the Grade 7 Practical Certificate.
**THEORY 3**

## Requirements & Marking

| Requirement | Total Marks |
|---|---|
| THREE LIST PIECES | |
| One from each of | |
| List A (Concerto) | 14 |
| List B (Sonata) | 12 |
| List C (Piece) | 12 |
| **EITHER** TWO STUDIES (6 marks each) | 12 |
| **OR** ONE STUDY AND ORCHESTRAL EXCERPTS | |
| ONE SUPPLEMENTARY PIECE | 8 |
| TECHNICAL TESTS | |
| Scales & Arpeggios | 16 |
| SIGHT READING | |
| Rhythm Pattern | 2 |
| Playing | 6 |
| AURAL TESTS | 8 |
| VIVA VOCE | 6 |
| MARKS FOR MEMORY | |
| List A and List C pieces only (2 marks each) | 4 |
| TOTAL POSSIBLE MARKS | 100 |

*NOTE: The examination program must include at least ONE work by a Canadian composer. The Canadian work may be chosen from the List Pieces OR as the Supplementary Piece. Candidates who fail to include a Canadian work will be subject to an automatic deduction from their over-all total mark.*

## Pieces

Candidates must be prepared to play TWO pieces from the list below, chosen to contrast in style, key, tempo, etc. Your choice must include TWO different composers. All pieces requiring accompaniment must be played with accompaniment. All pieces were available in print at the time the syllabus was prepared. Although suggested editions have been given below to assist candidates in identifying and purchasing music, ANY STANDARD EDITION may be used for the examination.

  * = *Canadian composer*

## LIST A

**RIEDING, O.**
Concertino in D, Op. 25 (1st mov't) — Bosworth
**SEITZ, F.**
Concerto No. 1 in D, Op. 7 — Any Edition
  CHOOSE EITHER 1st mov't to the Adagio section
  OR 3rd mov't, Allegretto in 6/8 to end
Concerto No. 3 in G minor, Op. 12 (1st mov't)
**SITT, H.**
Concerto in A minor, Opus 70 — Bosworth
  Play from beginning and end at the Animato (20 bars before
  Andante in 9/8)
**STAMITZ, J.**
Concerto in A minor (1st mov't) — Schott
**TELEMANN, G.P.**
Concerto in A minor (1st mov't) — Bosworth
**VIVALDI, A.**
Concerto in G minor, Op. 12 — Any Edition
  CHOOSE EITHER 1st OR 3rd movement

## LIST B

**ALBINONI, T.**
Sonata in A minor — Peters
  Choose ANY TWO contrasting movements
**CORELLI, A.**
Sonata in E, No. 11, Op. 5 — Peters
  Choose EITHER Preludio AND Allegro
  OR Preludio AND Vivace
**ECCLES, H.**
Sonata in G minor [orig. for Viola & Keyboard] — International
  Choose ANY TWO contrasting movements
**HÄNDEL, G. F.**
Sonata No. 6 in E — Peters
  Choose ANY TWO contrasting movements
**SENAILLE, J.-B.**
Sonata in D minor No. 4, Book IV — Any Edition
  1st mov't (Largo) AND final mov't (Allegro)
**TELEMANN, G. P.**
*6 Sonatas for Violin and Piano* — Schott
  Choose ANY ONE of
  Sonata 1 (Choose ANY TWO contrasting movements)
  Sonata 2 (Choose ANY TWO contrasting movements)
  Sonata 3 (Choose ANY TWO contrasting movements)
  Sonata 4 (Choose ANY TWO contrasting movements)
  Sonata 5 (Choose ANY TWO contrasting movements)
  Sonata 6 (Choose ANY TWO contrasting movements)
**VERACINI, F. M.**
Sonata in D minor — Fischer
  Choose ANY TWO contrasting movements
**\*WILLAN, H.**
Sonata No. 2 — Bosworth
  Largo AND Courante

## LIST C

**BÖHM, C.**
Perpetuum Mobile (*Little Suite*) — Fischer
Introduction and Polonaise — Fischer

**BOROWSKI, F.**
Adoration — Presser
**\*COUTTS, G.**
Hornpipe — Harris
**CUI, C.**
Orientale (*Kaleidoscope*), Op. 50, No. 9 — Schirmer
**DANCLA, J. B. C.**
Premier Solo — Peters
  (*Three Concert Solos for Violin and Piano, Op. 77*)
**DRDLA, F.**
Souvenir for Violin and Piano — Bosworth
**ELGAR, E.**
Salut d'amour Op. 12 (*Liebesgruss*) — Masters Music
  (*Three Pieces for Violin and Piano*)
**FIOCCO, G. H.**
La Legere — Schott
Allegro — Schott
**\*GRATTON, H.**
Chanson Ecossaise — Harris
Première dance canadienne — Harris
**GLUCK, C.W. (ARR. KREISLER)**
Melodie (*Orfeo et Euridice*) — Fischer
  (*The Fritz Kreisler Collection, Vol. 1*)
**\*HYSLOP, R.**
Haifa *(Bow Ties)* — Harris
Released *(Bow Ties)* — Harris
Red Shoes *(Bow Ties)* — Harris
**KREISLER, F.**
*The Fritz Kreisler Collection, Volume 1* — Fischer
  Choose ANY ONE of:
  Schon Rosmarin
  Liebeslied
*The Fritz Kreisler Collection, Volume 2* — Fischer
  Choose ANY ONE of:
  Andantino in the style of Martini
  Scherzo in the style of Dittersdorf
  March Miniature Viennoise
  Tempo di Minuetto in the style of Pugnani
Menuet in the style of Porpora — Foley/Fischer
**MENDELSSOHN, F. (ARR. KREISLER)**
Song without words, No. 1, Op. 62 — Fischer
  (*The Fritz Kreisler Collection, Vol. 1*)
**MOLLENHAUER, E.**
The Boy Paganini — Carl Fischer
**MLYNARSKI, E.**
Mazurka (*37 Pieces You Like to Play*) — Schirmer
**\*ROBINOVITCH, S.**
Adieu Babylon — CMC
**SCHUMANN, R.**
Fantasiestücke, Op. 73 — Schirmer
  No. 3 (in C)
**SEVERN, E.**
Polish Dance — Carl Fischer
**\*SHARMAN, R.**
Parahelia — CMC
**TOSELLI, E. (ARR. FRADKIN)**
Serenade, Op. 6 — Boston Music
**WIENIAWSKI, H.**
Kuiawiak (2nd Mazurka) — Carl Fischer

# Studies

Candidates must be prepared to play TWO contrasting studies in different keys. Memorization is recommended although NOT required.

---

Studies must be chosen as follows:

**EITHER** 1) Choose TWO Studies, one each from Study List A and Study List B, below.

**OR** 2) Choose ONE Study from either Study List A or Study List B, **AND** Orchestral Excerpts for Grade Seven Violin (see **Orchestral Excerpts**, below). This option is recommended for candidates who plan to continue working toward a professional music diploma or degree.

---

### STUDY LIST A

**TROTT, J.**
*Melodious Double Stops, Book 1*     Schirmer
Choose ANY ONE of
Nos. 21, 22, 23, 24, 25, 26, 27, 28, 29, 30

### STUDY LIST B

**MAZAS, J-F**
*75 Melodious & Progressive Studies, Op. 36, Book 1*     Schirmer
Choose ANY ONE of
Nos. 13, 15, 16, 17

**KREUTZER, R.**
*Forty-two Studies or Caprices for Violin*     Intl. *or* Schirmer
Choose ANY ONE of
Nos. 2, 3, 4, 5, 6

# Orchestral Excerpts (Optional)

Candidates choosing **OPTION 2)** in **Studies**, above, must be prepared to play ANY of the following orchestral excerpts, one or more of which will be chosen by the Examiner. Candidates should note that for each excerpt, they may be asked to start or stop in the middle of the excerpt passage. All excerpts can be found starting on page 56 of this syllabus. For those candidates who wish to prepare their excerpts from complete orchestral parts, please use the material at the back of this syllabus for reference.

**BACH, J. S.**
*Mass in B minor*
*Brandenburg Concerto No. 5 in D*

**HAYDN, F. J.**
*Symphony No. 31*
**SCHUBERT, F.**
*Symphony No. 8 in B minor ("Unfinished")*

# Supplementary Piece

Candidates must be prepared to play ONE Supplementary Piece. This piece need not be from the Syllabus lists, and may be chosen entirely at the discretion of the teacher and student. It may represent a period or style of piece not already included in the examination program, but which holds special interest for the candidate. The choice must be within the following guidelines:

1) The equivalent level of difficulty of the piece may be at a higher grade level, providing it is within the technical and musical grasp of the candidate.

2) Pieces below the equivalent of Grade 6 level are not acceptable.

3) The piece must be for solo violin (with or without piano accompaniment). Duets and trios are not acceptable.

4) Candidates with exceptional talent for improvisation may wish to improvise on a theme of their choice. In this case, items 1 and 2 (above) will apply. Marks will be given for originality, musical inventiveness, and structural unity.

Special approval is not required for the Supplementary Piece. However, poor suitability of the choice may be reflected in the mark. Memorization is encouraged, although NOT required.

## Technical Tests

All technical tests must be played from memory, evenly, with good tone, secure intonation, with all of the listed bowings, ascending and descending in the keys stated.

### SCALES

*ALL scales to be played from memory, ascending AND descending.*

|  | Keys | Octaves | Note Values | M.M. ♩= | Bowings |
|---|---|---|---|---|---|
| Major | **B, C** | 3 | ♪ | 60 |  |
| Harmonic Minor | **b, c** | 3 | ♪ | 60 |  |
| Melodic Minor | **b, c** | 3 | ♪ | 60 |  |
| Chromatic | **C, D** | 2 | ♪ | 92 |  |
| Double Stops in 3rds, 6ths, and ·8ves | **B, C** | 1 | 𝅗𝅥 | 84 | detaché – solid form (see example (a) below) |
| Broken Intervals/ Double Stops in 3rds 6ths, 8ves | **g melodic** | 1 | ♩ | 84 | (see note below) |

Example: a) double stops in 3rds, 6ths, and 8ves

*(see page 20 for examples of broken intervals / double stops in 3rds, 6ths, and 8ves)*

### ARPEGGIOS

*ALL arpeggios to be played from memory, ascending AND descending. Do NOT repeat the top note.*

|  | Keys | Octaves | Note Values | M.M. | Bowings Comments |
|---|---|---|---|---|---|
| Major | **B, C** | 3 | ♪♪♪ (triplet) | 80 |  |
| Minor | **b, c** | 3 | ♪♪♪ (triplet) | 80 |  |
| Dominant 7ths | In the keys of D, E♭ | 2 | ♪ | 80 |  |
| Diminished 7ths | In the keys of d, e♭ | 2 | ♪ | 80 |  |

## Sight Reading

Candidates are required to perform at sight a) a rhythmic exercise and b) a passage of violin score as described below. The candidate will be given a brief period to scan the score, but not to "practise silently" before beginning to play. Candidates must perform each section without counting aloud. It is recommended that candidates maintain a steady beat, and avoid the unnecessary repetition caused by attempting to correct errors during the performance.

| a) Rhythm | | b) Violin Passage | |
|---|---|---|---|
| To tap, clap or play on one note (at the candidate's choice) a simple rhythm. | | To play at sight a simple melody, about equal in difficulty to pieces of Grade 5 level. | |
| Length | 4 bars | Keys | Major & Minor up to and |
| Time signature | 2/4, 3/4, 6/8 | | including 3 sharps or flats |
| Note values | variety of values including ties | Length | 8-16 bars |
| Rest values | variety of values | | |

Example a) Rhythm

## Aural Tests

The candidate will be required:

i) at the candidate's choice, to play back OR sing back to any vowel, a short melody of six to eight notes, in 2/4, 3/4, 4/4, or 6/8 time, based on the first six notes and the lower leading tone in a *major* or *minor* key, after the Examiner has:
- ✓ named the key [up to and including three sharps or flats]
- ✓ played the 4-note chord on the tonic in broken form
- ✓ played the melody twice.

The melody will begin on the tonic note. Only the harmonic form of the minor will be used. Following is the approximate level of difficulty:

ii) to identify any of the following intervals after each one has been played once by the Examiner in broken form:

| ABOVE a note | BELOW a note |
|---|---|
| *major and minor 2nd* | *major and minor 3rd* |
| *major and minor 3rd* | *perfect 4th* |
| *perfect 4th* | *perfect 5th* |
| *perfect 5th* | *major and minor 6th* |
| *major and minor 6th* | *perfect octave* |
| *minor 7th* | |
| *perfect octave* | |

iii) to identify any of the following triads/chords when played once by the Examiner in solid form, in close, root position:
*major* and *minor* triads (3-note)
*augmented* triads (3-note)
*dominant 7th* chords (4-note)
*diminished 7th* chords (4-note)

iv) to state whether a short piece in *chorale* style is in a *major* or a *minor* key, and whether the final cadence is **Perfect** (V-I), **Imperfect** (I-V only), **Plagal** (IV-I), or **Interrupted/Deceptive** (V-VI).

# Viva Voce

Candidates must be prepared to give verbal answers to questions on the THREE List pieces selected for the examination. Candidates must ensure that all teaching notes and other written comments are removed from the score before the examination. The questions will include the following elements:

i)    to find and explain all of the signs (including clefs, time signatures, key signatures, accidentals, etc.), articulation markings (legato, staccato, accents, phrase or slur markings, etc.), dynamic and tempo markings, and other musical terms as they may be found in the THREE selected pieces.

ii)   without reference to the score, to give the title, key and composer of the piece.

iii)  to explain the meaning of the title of the piece.

iv)   to give a few relevant details about the composer.

v)    with direct reference to the score, to explain briefly the form of the piece (for example, binary or ternary form, dance piece, sonata, etc.)

vi)   with direct reference to the score, to explain briefly the key structure, including any modulations.

*NOTE: Candidates taking a Partial Examination MUST include Viva Voce on the partial that includes the LAST List Piece, and*
> *i)    be prepared to answer questions on ALL THREE List Pieces;*
> *ii)   provide music for ALL THREE List Pieces.*

---

# GRADE EIGHT

Length of the examination:    40 minutes

Examination Fee:    Please consult the current examination application form for the schedule of fees.

Co-requisite:    Successful completion of the following written examination is required for the awarding of the Grade 8 Practical Certificate.
**THEORY 4**

## Requirements & Marking

| Requirement | Total Marks |
|---|---|
| FOUR LIST PIECES | |
| One from each of | |
| List A (Concerto) | 13 |
| List B (Sonata) | 10 |
| List C (Piece) | 10 |
| List D (Unaccompanied) | 10 |
| **EITHER** TWO STUDIES (6 marks each) | 12 |
| **OR** ONE STUDY AND ORCHESTRAL EXCERPTS | |
| ONE SUPPLEMENTARY PIECE | 8 |
| TECHNICAL TESTS | |
| Scales & Arpeggios | 14 |
| SIGHT READING | |
| Rhythm Pattern | 2 |
| Playing | 6 |
| AURAL TESTS | 8 |
| VIVA VOCE (List Pieces only) | 4 |
| MARKS FOR MEMORY | 3 |
| List A, List C, and List D pieces only (1 mark each) | |
| TOTAL POSSIBLE MARKS | 100 |

*NOTE: The examination program must include at least ONE work by a Canadian composer. The Canadian work may be chosen from the List Pieces OR as the Supplementary Piece. Candidates who fail to include a Canadian work will be subject to an automatic deduction from their over-all total mark.*

## Pieces

Candidates must be prepared to play TWO pieces from the list below, chosen to contrast in style, key, tempo, etc. Your choice must include TWO different composers. All pieces requiring accompaniment must be played with accompaniment. All pieces were available in print at the time the syllabus was prepared. Although suggested editions have been given below to assist candidates in identifying and purchasing music, ANY STANDARD EDITION may be used for the examination.

\* = *Canadian composer*

## LIST A

**ACCOLAY, J-B**
Concertino No. 1 in A minor (complete)                    Kalmus
Concertino No. 3 in E minor (complete)                    Kalmus
**BACH, J. S.**
Concerto in A minor, BWV 1041 (1st mov't)         Any Edition
**HAYDN, F. J.**
Concerto in G, Hob.VIIa/4*                          Any Edition
(1st mov't with cadenza)
**NARDINI, P.**
Concerto in E minor                                International
Choose EITHER 1st AND 2nd movements
OR 2nd AND 3rd movements
**RIEDING, O.**
Concerto in E minor, Op. 7                           Bosworth
play from beginning to end of cadenza then cut and play 14th
measure after Meno mosso to end

## LIST B

**BACH, J. S.**
Sonata No. 4 in C minor, BWV 1017 (*6 Sonatas*)     Any Edition
Choose ANY TWO contrasting movements
Sonata No. 5 in F minor, BWV 1018 (*6 Sonatas*)     Any Edition
Choose ANY TWO contrasting movements
Sonata No. 6 in G, BWV 1019 (*6 Sonatas*)           Any Edition
Choose ANY TWO contrasting movements
**CORELLI, A.**
Sonatas for Violin and Piano, Op. 5                    Peters
Choose ANY ONE of
Sonata No. 1 (Choose ANY TWO contrasting movements)
Sonata No. 2 (Choose ANY TWO contrasting movements)
Sonata No. 3 (Choose ANY TWO contrasting movements)
Sonata No. 4 (Choose ANY TWO contrasting movements)
Sonata No. 5 (Choose ANY TWO contrasting movements)
Sonata No. 6 (Choose ANY TWO contrasting movements)

## LIST C

**BACH, J. S. (ARR. WILHELMJ)**
Celebrated Air on the G String                         Fischer
***CHAMPAGNE, C.**
Danse Villageoise (Country Dance)                     Berandol
**DANCLA, J. B. C.**
*Three Concert Solos for Violin and Piano, Op. 77*       Peters
Choose ANY ONE of
Deuxième Solo
Troisième Solo
**DVORÁK, A.**
Ballad, Op. 15 (*Three Pieces for Violin*)             Schirmer
***FODI, J.**
3 Pieces                                                 CMC
***GIRON, A.**
*Six Studies*                                            CMC
Choose ANY ONE of
Rodentia
Gypsy
Skedaddle
**GODOWSKI, L. (ARR. HEIFETZ)**
Alt-Wien                                       Schirmer or Fischer
**GRANADOS, E. (ARR. KREISLER)**
Spanish Dance in E minor                               Fischer
(*The Fritz Kreisler Collection Volume 1*)
**HUBAY, J.**
Bolero                                                 Bosworth

***JAQUE, R.**
Petit Air Roumain                                        CMC
Spiccato et legato                                       CMC
***KOLINSKI, M.**
Little Suite for Violin and Piano                        CMC
Choose ANY ONE movement
**KREISLER, F.**
*The Fritz Kreisler Collection Volume 1*               Fischer
La Gitana
Sicilienne and Rigaudon in the style of Françoeur
*The Fritz Kreisler Collection Volume 2*               Fischer
The Old Refrain
Polichinelle
Syncopation
**ᴬLIADOV, D.**
Prelude                                                  CMC
**MASSENET, J.**
Meditation from "Thaïs"                            United Music
**MONTI, V.**
Csardas                                         Fischer/Ricordi
**POULENC, F. (ARR. HEIFETZ)**
Mouvements Perpetuels                                  Fischer
**RAVEL, M.**
Pièce en forme de Habanera                              Leduc
**SCHUBERT, F.**
The Bee, No. 9, Op. 13                                 Fischer
**STRAVINSKY, I. (TRANSCR. DUSHKIN)**
Chanson Russe (Russian Maiden's Song)       Boosey & Hawkes
**SVENDSEN, J. S.**
Romanze, Op. 26                                         Peters
***TELFER, N.**
Landscapes                                               CMC
Choose EITHER I and II OR III and IV
**WIENIAWSKI, H.**
Obertass, Op. 19 (Mazurka)                             Fischer

## LIST D

**BACH, J. S.**
*Six Sonatas and Partitas for Solo Violin*              Schott
Partita No. 2 in D minor, BWV 1004
Choose ANY ONE of
Courante
Gigue
Partita No. 3 in E, BWV 1006
Choose ANY ONE of
Bouree
Gigue
**PAGANINI, N. (ED. DEVICH)**
*60 Variations sur l'air Barucaba pour Violon (solo) Op. 14*  EMB
Choose EITHER (a) OR (b)
(a) No. 1 AND No. 2 AND No. 3
(b) No. 7 AND No. 8 AND No. 9
The theme before No. 1 and the "finis" after No. 60 should
be played at the beginning and end of each group of
Variations, in the appropriate keys
**TELEMANN, G. P. (ED. GINGOLD)**
*Twelve Fantasias for Solo Violin*                 International
No. 1 Largo
No. 2 Largo and final Allegro with repeats
No. 9 Siciliana and Vivace
No. 10 Presto OR Largo and Allegro
**WIENIAWSKI, H. (ED. GINGOLD)**
Etudes-Caprices, Op. 18 for Solo Violin           International
No. 1 Allegro Moderato only

# Studies

Candidates must be prepared to play TWO contrasting studies in different keys. Memorization is recommended although NOT required

---

Studies must be chosen as follows:

**EITHER** 1) Choose TWO Studies, one each from Study List A and Study List B, below.

**OR** 2) Choose ONE Study from either Study List A or Study List B, **AND** Orchestral Excerpts for Grade Eight Violin (see **Orchestral Excerpts**, below). This option is recommended for candidates who plan to continue working toward a professional music diploma or degree.

---

### STUDY LIST A

**MAZAS, J-F**
*75 Melodious & Progressive Studies, Op. 36, Book 1*    Schirmer
Choose ANY ONE of
Nos. 25, 26, 28, 29, 30
*75 Melodious & Progressive Studies, Op. 36, Book 2*    Schirmer
Choose ANY ONE of
Nos. 37, 38, 39, 40

### STUDY LIST B

**DONT, J.**
*Twenty-Four Etudes and Caprices, Op. 35*    Schirmer
Choose ANY ONE of
Nos. 3, 5, 6, 7, 9
**KREUTZER, R.**
*Forty-two Studies or Caprices for Violin*    International/Schirmer
Choose ANY ONE of
Nos. 1, 12, 13, 14, 15, 16, 17

# Orchestral Excerpts (Optional)

Candidates choosing **OPTION 2)** in **Studies**, above, must be prepared to play ALL of the following orchestral excerpts, one or more of which will be chosen by the Examiner. Candidates should note that for each excerpt, they may be asked to start or stop in the middle of the excerpt passage. All excerpts can be found starting on page 56 of this syllabus. For those candidates who wish to prepare their excerpts from complete orchestral parts, please use the material at the back of this syllabus for reference.

**BACH, J. S.**
*Brandenburg Concerto No. 1 in F*
*St. Matthew Passion*

**HAYDN, F. J.**
*Symphony No. 101 in D ("Clock")*
**MOZART, W. A.**
*Symphony No. 38 in D ("Prague"), K.504*

# Supplementary Piece

Candidates must be prepared to play ONE Supplementary Piece. This piece need not be from the Syllabus lists, and may be chosen entirely at the discretion of the teacher and student. It may represent a period or style of piece not already included in the examination program, but which holds special interest for the candidate. The choice must be within the following guidelines:

1) The equivalent level of difficulty of the piece may be at a higher grade level, providing it is within the technical and musical grasp of the candidate.

2) Pieces below the equivalent of Grade 7 level are not acceptable.

3) The piece must be for solo violin (with or without piano accompaniment). Duets and trios are not acceptable.

4) Candidates with exceptional talent for improvisation may wish to improvise on a theme of their choice. In this case, items 1 and 2 (above) will apply. Marks will be given for originality, musical inventiveness, and structural unity.

Special approval is not required for the Supplementary Piece. However, poor suitability of the choice may be reflected in the mark. Memorization is encouraged, although NOT required.

## Technical Tests

All technical tests must be played from memory, evenly, with good tone, secure intonation, with all of the listed bowings, ascending and descending in the keys stated.

### SCALES

*ALL scales to be played from memory, ascending AND descending.*

|  | Keys | Octaves | Note Values | M.M. ♩= | Bowings Comments |
|---|---|---|---|---|---|
| Major | B♭, D, E♭ | 3 | ♪ | 66 | 8 or 12 slurred |
| Melodic Minor | b♭, d, e♭ | 3 | ♪ | 66 | 8 or 12 slurred |
| Harmonic Minor | b♭, d, e♭ | 3 | ♪ | 66 | 8 or 12 slurred |
| Chromatic | E♭ | 2 | ♪ | 66 | 12 slurred; 1 8ᵛᵉ per bow |
| Double Stops in 3ʳᵈˢ | B♭, C<br>b♭, c melodic | 2 | ♩ | 66 | detaché |
| Double Stops in 6ᵗʰˢ | B♭, C<br>b♭, c melodic | 2 | ♩ | 66 | detaché |
| Double Stops in 8ᵛᵉˢ | B♭, C<br>b♭, c melodic | 2 | ♩ | 66 | detaché |
| Artificial Harmonics | B♭, C<br>b♭, c melodic | 1 | ♩ | 66 | detaché<br>quads only |

### ARPEGGIOS

*ALL arpeggios to be played from memory, ascending AND descending. Do NOT repeat the top note.*

|  | Keys | Octaves | Note Values | M.M. | Bowings Comments |
|---|---|---|---|---|---|
| Major | B♭, D, E♭ | 3 | ♫♩ (triplet) | 72 | 3 8ᵛᵉ per bow |
| Minor | b♭, d, e♭ | 3 | ♫♩ (triplet) | 72 | 3 8ᵛᵉ per bow |
| Dominant 7ths | In the keys of E♭, F | 2 | ♪ | 84 | (slurred groups of 4) |
| Diminished 7ths | In the keys of e, g | 2 | ♪ | 84 | (slurred groups of 4) |

## Sight Reading

Candidates are required to perform at sight a) a rhythmic exercise and b) a passage of violin score as described below. The candidate will be given a brief period to scan the score, but not to "practise silently" before beginning to play. Candidates must perform each section without counting aloud. It is recommended that candidates maintain a steady beat, and avoid the unnecessary repetition caused by attempting to correct errors during the performance.

| a) Rhythm | | b) Violin Passage | |
|---|---|---|---|
| To tap or play on one note (at the candidate's choice) a rhythm in simple or compound time. May include syncopated rhythms. | | To play at sight a melody, about equal in difficulty to pieces of Grade 6 level. | |
| Length | 4-8 bars | Keys | Major & Minor up to and including 5 sharps or flats |
| Time signature | any simple OR compound time | Length | 8-16 bars |
| Note values | variety of values including triplets and ties | | |
| Rest values | variety of values | | |

Example a) Rhythm

## Aural Tests

The candidate will be required:

i)    at the candidate's choice, to play back OR sing back to any vowel a short melody of eight to twelve notes, in 2/4, 3/4, 4/4 or 6/8 time, in a *major* or *minor* key, within the range of one octave, after the Examiner has:
- ✓ named the key [up to three sharps or flats]
- ✓ played the 4-note chord on the tonic [broken form]
- ✓ played the melody twice.

The melody may begin on ANY note of the tonic chord. Only the harmonic form of the minor will be used. Following is the approximate level of difficulty:

ii)    to identify any of the following intervals after the Examiner has played each one once in broken form:

| **ABOVE a note** | **BELOW a note** |
|---|---|
| *major and minor 2nd* | *major and minor 2nd* |
| *major and minor 3rd* | *major and minor 3rd* |
| *perfect 4th* | *perfect 4th* |
| *perfect 5th* | *perfect 5th* |
| *major and minor 6th* | *major and minor 6th* |
| *major and minor 7th* | *major and minor 7th* |
| *perfect octave* | *perfect octave* |

iii)    to identify any of the following triads/chords when played once by the Examiner in solid form, in close, root position:

       *major* and *minor* triads (3-note)
       *augmented* triads (3-note)
       *diminished* triads (3-note)
       *dominant 7th* chords (4-note)
       *diminished 7th* chords (4-note)

iv) to state whether a short piece in *chorale* style is in a *major* or a *minor* key, and whether both the final AND one internal cadence are **Perfect** (V-I), **Imperfect** (1-V, II-V, and IV-V), **Plagal** (IV-I), or **Interrupted/Deceptive** (V-VI). The Examiner will play the passage TWICE; the first time straight through without interruption, the second time stopping at the internal cadence point for the candidate to identify it.

## Viva Voce

Candidates must be prepared to give verbal answers to questions on the FOUR List pieces selected for the examination. Candidates must ensure that all teaching notes and other written comments are removed from the score before the examination. The questions will include the following elements:

i) to find and explain all of the signs (including clefs, time signatures, key signatures, accidentals, etc.), articulation markings (legato, staccato, accents, phrase or slur markings, etc.), dynamic and tempo markings, and other musical terms as they may be found in the four selected pieces.

ii) without reference to the score, to give the title, key and composer of the piece.

iii) to explain the meaning of the title of the piece.

iv) to give a few relevant details about the composer.

v) with direct reference to the score, to explain briefly the form of the piece (for example, binary or ternary form, dance piece, sonata, etc.)

vi) with direct reference to the score, to explain briefly the key structure, including any modulations.

*NOTE: Candidates taking a Partial Examination MUST include Viva Voce on the partial that includes the LAST List Piece, and*
       *i)   be prepared to answer questions on ALL FOUR List Pieces;*
       *ii)  provide music for ALL FOUR List Pieces.*

---

# GRADE NINE

Length of the examination:     40 minutes

Examination Fee:             Please consult the current examination application form for the schedule of fees.

Co-requisites:                Successful completion of the following written examination is required for the awarding of the Grade 9 Practical Certificate.
**THEORY 5** AND **HISTORY 5 OR HISTORY 6**

## Requirements & Marking

| Requirement | Total Marks |
|---|---|
| FOUR LIST PIECES | |
| One from each of | |
|     List A (Concerto) | 14 |
|     List B (Sonata) | 10 |
|     List C (Piece) | 10 |
|     List D (Unaccompanied) | 9 |
| TWO STUDIES (5 marks each) | 10 |
| ORCHESTRAL EXCERPTS | 6 |
| ONE SUPPLEMENTARY PIECE | 8 |
| TECHNICAL TESTS | |
|     Scales & Arpeggios | 14 |
| SIGHT READING | |
|     Rhythm Pattern | 2 |
|     Playing | 6 |
| AURAL TESTS | 8 |
| MARKS FOR MEMORY | |
| List A, List C and List D pieces only (1 mark each) | 3 |
| TOTAL POSSIBLE MARKS | 100 |

*NOTE: The examination program must include at least ONE work by a Canadian composer. The Canadian work may be chosen from the List Pieces OR as the Supplementary Piece. Candidates who fail to include a Canadian work will be subject to an automatic deduction from their over-all total mark.*

## Pieces

Candidates must be prepared to play TWO pieces from the list below, chosen to contrast in style, key, tempo, etc. Your choice must include TWO different composers. All pieces requiring accompaniment must be played with accompaniment. All pieces were available in print at the time the syllabus was prepared. Although suggested editions have been given below to assist candidates in identifying and purchasing music, ANY STANDARD EDITION may be used for the examination

    * = *Canadian composer*

## LIST A

**BACH, J. S.**
Concerto in E — Any Edition
  Choose EITHER 1st mov't OR 3rd mov't
**DE BERIOT, CHARLES**
Concerto No. 7 in G, Op. 76 — Fischer
  Choose EITHER 1st mov't OR 3rd mov't
Concerto No. 9 in A minor, Op. 104 — Schirmer
  Choose ANY ONE of
    1st AND 2nd mov'ts
    2nd AND 3rd mov'ts
**HAYDN, F. J.**
Concerto in C Hob. VII:1 — Henle
  1st mov't with cadenza
Concerto in A Hob. VIIa:3 — Henle
  1st mov't with cadenza
**MOZART, W. A.**
Concerto in D ("Adelaide") (1st mov't) — Any Edition
Concerto in G, K. 216 (1st mov't with Franko cadenza) — Schirmer
**RODE, P.**
Concerto No. 7 in A minor, Op. 9 — Schirmer
  Choose ANY ONE of
    1st AND 2nd mov'ts (Allegro molto AND Adagio)
    3rd mov't (Allegro moderato)
**SPOHR, L.**
Concerto No. 8 in A minor, Op. 47 — Any Edition
  Choose EITHER 1st AND 2nd movements
  OR 3rd movement
**VIVALDI, A.**
*Four Seasons* — Any Edition
  "Spring" (complete)

## LIST B

**BEETHOVEN, L. VAN**
Sonata No. 1 in D, Op. 12 (1st mov't) — Peters
Sonata No. 2 in A, Op. 12 (1st mov't) — Peters
Sonata No. 5 in F, Op. 24 ("Spring") (1st mov't) — Peters
***BUCZYNSKI, W.**
Sonata, Op. 1979 (1st mov't) — CMC
**COPLAND, A.**
Sonata for Violin and Piano — Boosey & Hawkes
  Choose ANY ONE of
    1st mov't (Andante semplice)
    3rd mov't (Allegretto giusto)
***GIRON, A.**
Sonata for Violin and Piano — CMC
  Choose ANY TWO contrasting movements
**HINDEMITH, P.**
Sonata in E (complete) — Masters Music OR Schott
**MOZART, W. A.**
Sonata No. 7 in F, K. 376 (1st AND 2nd mov'ts) — Any edition
Sonata No. 8 in C, K. 296 (1st AND 2nd mov'ts) — Any edition
Sonata No. 9 in F, K. 377 (1st AND 2nd mov'ts) — Any edition
**TARTINI, G.**
Sonata in G minor ("Didone Abbandonata") — Any edition
  Choose ANY TWO contrasting movements
**VIVALDI, A.**
Sonata in D major (arr. Respighi) — Ricordi
  1st mov't AND 2nd mov't
***WILLAN, H.**
Sonata No. 1 in E minor (1st mov't) — Berandol/BMI

## LIST C

**BARTOK, B. (TRANS. SZEKELY)**
Roumanian Folk Dances — Universal

**BEETHOVEN, L. VAN**
*Romantzen für Violine und Klavier* — Peters
  Romanze in F, Op. 50
**CORELLI, A.**
La Folia — Schirmer
**DE BERIOT, C.**
Scene de Ballet (Fantasia), Op. 100 — Fischer
**DEBUSSY, C. (ARR. HARTMANN)**
La Fille aux Cheveux de Lin — Editions Durand
**DVORÁK, A.**
Nocturne, Op. 40 (*Three Pieces for Violin and Piano*) — Schirmer
Romance in F minor, Op. 11 (arr. Gingold) — International
**GRANADOS, E.**
Spanish Dances No. 5 "Andaluza" — Union Musical Española
***GRATTON, H.**
Quatrième danse canadienne — Berandol
***HEALEY, D.**
Machere — CMC
***HOLT, P.E.**
Pastorale and Finale — CMC
**KREISLER, F.**
Liebesfreud — Foley
***LEUDEKE, R.**
Fancy #5 (*Fancies and Interludes*) — CMC
***RAMINSH, I.**
Aria for Violin and Piano — CMC
**RIES, F.**
Perpetuum Mobile, No. 5, Op. 34 — International
**RACHMANINOFF, S.**
Vocalise, No. 14, Op. 34 — International
**RIMSKY-KORSAKOV, N. (TRANS. HEIFETZ)**
The Bumble Bee (*The Legend of Tsar Saltan*) — Fischer
**SARASATE, P. DE**
Playera, No. 1, Op. 23 — International
Habañera, No. 2, Op. 21 — International
Les Adieux, Op. 9 — Fischer
**SCHUBERT, F. (TRANS. WILHELMJ)**
Ave Maria for Violin and Piano (ed. Heifetz) — Fischer
**TCHAIKOVSKY, P. I.**
Valse Sentimentale, No. 6, Op. 51 — Schirmer
  (*Two Sentimental Pieces*)
*Three Pieces for Violin and Piano, Op. 42* — International
  Choose ANY ONE of
    No. 1 – Meditation
    No. 2 – Scherzo
    No. 3 – Melodie
**VIEUXTEMPS, H.**
Ballade and Polonaise, Op. 38 — Fischer
Legende, Op. 17 — Fischer

## LIST D

**BACH, J. S.**
*Six Sonatas and Partitas for Solo Violin* — International
  Choose ANY ONE of
    Partita No. 1 in B minor, BWV 1002
      Sarabande AND Double)
    Partita No. 2 in D minor, BWV 1004
      Choose EITHER Allemande OR Gigue
    Sonata No. 3 in C, BWV 1005
      Allegro Assai
    Partita No. 3 in E, BWV 1006
      Choose EITHER Gavotte en Rondeau
      OR Menuet 1 AND Menuet 2

**PAGANINI, N.**
*60 Variations sur l'air Barucaba pour Violon (solo) Op. 14*  EMB
Choose EITHER (a) OR (b)
(a) No. 10 and No. 11 and No. 12 and No. 13
(b) No. 14 and No. 18 and No. 19 and No. 23
The theme before No. 1 and the "finis" after No. 60 should
be played at the beginning and end of each group of
Variations, in the appropriate keys

**TELEMANN, G. P. (ED. GINGOLD)**
*Twelve Fantasies for Solo Violin*                    International
Choose ANY ONE of
Fantasie No. 4
Fantasie No. 5
Fantasie No. 6
**WIENIAWSKI, H. (ED. GINGOLD)**
· *Etudes and Caprices for Solo Violin, Op. 18*        International
No. 3

## Studies

Candidates must be prepared to play TWO contrasting studies in different keys, ONE from Study List A and ONE
from Study List B, below.  Memorization is recommended although NOT required.

### STUDY LIST A

**MAZAS, J-F**
*75 Melodious & Progressive Studies, Op. 36 Book 2*   Schirmer
Choose ANY ONE of
Nos. 55, 56, 57

### STUDY LIST B

**DONT, J.**
*Twenty-Four Etudes and Caprices, Op. 35*             Schirmer
Choose ANY ONE of
Nos. ,10, 11, 12, 13, 14, 17, 18
**FIORILLO, F.**
*Thirty-Six Etudes and Caprices for Violin*    International/Fischer
Choose ANY ONE of
Nos. 2, 3, 5, 15, 18, 21
**KREUTZER, R.**
*Forty-two Studies or Caprices for Violin*        Intl. *or* Schirmer
Choose ANY ONE of
Nos. 18, 20, 22, 24

## Orchestral Excerpts

Candidates must be prepared to play ANY of the following orchestral excerpts, one or more of which will be chosen
by the Examiner.  Candidates should note that for each excerpt, they may be asked to start or stop in the middle of
the excerpt passage. All excerpts can be found starting on page 56 of this syllabus.  For those candidates who wish
to prepare their excerpts from complete orchestral parts, please use the material at the back of this syllabus for
reference.

**BEETHOVEN, L. VAN**
*Overture "Prometheus", Op. 43*
**BRAHMS, J.**
*Symphony No, 2 in D, Op. 73*

**HAYDN, F. J.**
*Symphony No. 103*
**VAUGHAN WILLIAMS, R.**
*Fantasia on a Theme by Tallis*

## Supplementary Piece

Candidates must be prepared to play ONE Supplementary Piece.  This piece need not be from the Syllabus lists, and
may be chosen entirely at the discretion of the teacher and student. It may represent a period or style of piece not
already included in the examination program, but which holds special interest for the candidate. The choice must be
within the following guidelines:

1)  The equivalent level of difficulty of the piece may be at a higher grade level, providing it is within the
technical and musical grasp of the candidate.

2)  Pieces below the equivalent of Grade 8 level are not acceptable.

3)  The piece must be for solo violin (with or without piano accompaniment). Duets and trios are not
acceptable.

4)   Candidates with exceptional talent for improvisation may wish to improvise on a theme of their choice. In this case, items 1 and 2 (above) will apply. Marks will be given for originality, musical inventiveness, and structural unity.

Special approval is not required for the Supplementary Piece.  However, poor suitability of the choice may be reflected in the mark. Memorization is encouraged, although NOT required.

## Technical Tests

All technical tests must be played from memory, evenly, with good tone, secure intonation, with all of the listed bowings, ascending and descending in the keys stated.

### SCALES

*ALL scales to be played from memory, ascending AND descending.*

|  | Keys | Octaves | Note Values | M.M. ♩= | Bowings |
|---|---|---|---|---|---|
| Major | D♭, E, F | 3 | ♪ | 72 | 8 <u>and</u> 12 slurred |
| Melodic Minor | d♭, e, f | 3 | ♪ | 72 | 8 <u>and</u> 12 slurred |
| Harmonic Minor | d♭, e, f | 3 | ♪ | 72 | 8 <u>and</u> 12 slurred |
| Chromatic | A, C | 3 | ♪ | 72 | 12 slurred |
| Double Stops in 3rds | A, D, E <br> a, d, e harmonic <br> & melodic | 2 | ♩ | 72 | detaché |
| Double Stops in 6ths | A, D, E <br> a, d, e harmonic <br> & melodic | 2 <br> 1 | ♩ | 72 | detaché |
| Double Stops in 8ves | A, D, E <br> a, d, e harmonic <br> & melodic | 2 <br> 1 | ♩ | 72 | detaché |
| Artificial Harmonics | A♭, A | 2 | ♩ | 72 | detaché <br> quads only |

### ARPEGGIOS

*ALL arpeggios to be played from memory, ascending AND descending.  Do NOT repeat the top note.*

|  | Keys | Octaves | Note Values | M.M. | Bowings Comments |
|---|---|---|---|---|---|
| Major | D♭, E, F | 3 | ♪♪♪ (triplet) | 88 | 3 8ve per bow |
| Minor | d♭, e, f | 3 | ♪♪♪ (triplet) | 88 | 3 8ve per bow |
| Dominant 7ths | In the keys of G, A, B | 2 | ♪ | 88 | ♩♪♪♪ ♩♪♪♪ |
| Diminished 7ths | In the keys of a♭, b♭ | 2 | ♪ | 88 | ♪♪♪♪ ♪♪♪♪ |

## Sight Reading

Candidates are required to perform at sight a) a rhythmic exercise and b) a passage of violin score as described below.  The candidate will be given a brief period to scan the score, but not to "practise silently" before beginning to play. Candidates must perform each section without counting aloud. It is recommended that candidates maintain a steady beat, and avoid the unnecessary repetition caused by attempting to correct errors during the performance.

| *a) Rhythm* | *b) Violin Passage* |
|---|---|
| To tap, clap or play on one note (at the candidate's choice) a rhythm in simple or compound time. May include syncopated rhythms, changing meters, and complex patterns, but not irregular meters. | To play at sight a melody, about equal in difficulty to pieces of Grade 7 level. |
|    Length           4 bars |    Keys          Major & Minor up to and including 5 sharps or flats |
|    Time signature   any simple OR compound time |    Length     16-24 bars |
|    Note values    variety of values including ties | |
| Rest values       variety of values | |

Example a) Rhythm

## Aural Tests

The candidate will be required:

i) at the candidate's choice, to play back OR sing back to any vowel, the **upper** part of a two-part phrase in a major key, after the Examiner has:

    ✓ named the key [up to three sharps or flats]
    ✓ played the 4-note chord on the tonic [solid form]
    ✓ played the passage twice.

The parts may begin on ANY note of the tonic chord. Following is the approximate level of difficulty:

ii) to identify any of the following intervals after the Examiner has played each one once in broken form:

| **ABOVE a note** | **BELOW a note** |
|---|---|
| *major and minor 2nd* | *major and minor 2nd* |
| *major and minor 3rd* | *major and minor 3rd* |
| *perfect 4th* | *perfect 4th* |
| *augmented 4th (diminished 5th)* | *augmented 4th (diminished 5th)* |
| *perfect 5th* | *perfect 5th* |
| *major and minor 6th* | *major and minor 6th* |
| *major and minor 7th* | *major and minor 7th* |
| *perfect octave* | *perfect octave* |

iii) to identify any of the following 4-note chords, and name the position, after each has been played once by the Examiner:

    *major* and *minor* chords: root position or first inversion [to be played solid form, close position]
    *dominant 7th* chords: root position only [to be played in solid form, open (SATB) position]
    *diminished 7th* chords: root position only [to be played in solid form, open (SATB) position]

iv) to state whether a short piece in *chorale* style is in a *major* or a *minor* key, and whether the final cadence and any internal cadences are **Perfect** (V-I), **Imperfect** (I-V, II-V, IV-V), **Plagal** (IV-I), or **Interrupted/Deceptive** (V-VI). The Examiner will play the passage TWICE; the first time straight through without interruption, the second time stopping at cadence points for the candidate to identify them.

# GRADE TEN

Length of the examination:    55 minutes

Examination Fee:    Please consult the current examination application form for the schedule of fees.

Co-requisites:    Successful completion of the following written examination is required for the awarding of the Grade 10 Practical Certificate.
**THEORY 6** AND **HISTORY 5** AND **HISTORY 6**

*Note:   Completion of Grade 10 is NOT required to proceed to the Associate Diploma. However, candidates who successfully complete Grade 10 will be exempt from the Associate Diploma technique providing they obtain a minimum total of 70% in each of Technical Tests, Sight Reading and Aural Tests.*

## Requirements & Marking

| Requirement | Total Marks |
|---|---|
| FOUR LIST PIECES | |
| To be performed from memory, one from each of | |
| List A (Concerto) | 13 |
| List B (Sonata) | 12 |
| List C (Piece) | 11 |
| List D (Unaccompanied) | 10 |
| TWO STUDIES (5 marks each) | 10 |
| ORCHESTRAL EXCERPTS | 6 |
| ONE SUPPLEMENTARY PIECE | 8 |
| TECHNICAL TESTS | |
| Scales & Arpeggios | 14 |
| SIGHT READING | |
| Rhythm Pattern | 2 |
| Playing | 6 |
| AURAL TESTS | 8 |
| TOTAL POSSIBLE MARKS | 100 |

***NOTE: The examination program must include at least ONE work by a Canadian composer. The Canadian work may be chosen from the List Pieces OR as the Supplementary Piece. Candidates who fail to include a Canadian work will be subject to an automatic deduction from their over-all total mark.***

## Pieces

Candidates must be prepared to play TWO pieces from the list below, chosen to contrast in style, key, tempo, etc. Your choice must include TWO different composers. All pieces requiring accompaniment must be played with accompaniment. All pieces must be performed from memory. All pieces were available in print at the time the syllabus was prepared. Although suggested editions have been given below to assist candidates in identifying and purchasing music, ANY STANDARD EDITION may be used for the examination

## GRADE 10

*= *Canadian composer*

### LIST A

**BRUCH, M.**
Concerto in G minor, Op. 26 (1st AND 2nd mov'ts)  Any edition
**HAYDN, F. J.**
Concerto in B, Hob.VIIa:B2 (1st mov't with cadenza)  Breitkopf
**KABALEVSKY, D.**
Concerto in C, Op. 48 (1st AND 2nd mov'ts)  International
**MOZART, W. A.**
Concerto No. 4 in D, K. 218  International
1st AND 2nd mov'ts with cadenzas
**SPOHR, L.**
Concerto No. 6 in G minor, Op. 28 (1st mov't)  Fischer
**VIOTTI, G. B.**
Concerto No. XXII in A minor (1st mov't AND cadenza)  Schirmer
**VIVALDI, A.**
*Four Seasons*  Any edition
Choose ANY ONE of
Autumn (complete)
Summer (complete)
Winter (complete)
*****WEINZWEIG, J.**
Concerto Op. 22  Carisch
(1st mov't and ANY ONE other contrasting mov't)

### LIST B

**BEETHOVEN, L. VAN**
Sonata No. 3 in E flat, Op. 12 (1st mov't)  Any edition
Sonata No. 1 in A, Op. 30 (1st mov't)  Any edition
Sonata No. 2 in C minor, Op. 30 (1st mov't)  Any edition
Sonata No. 3 in G, Op. 30 (1st mov't)  Any edition
**BRAHMS, J.**
Sonata No. 1 in G, Op. 78 (1st mov't)  Henle
Sonata No. 2 in A, Op. 100 (1st mov't)  Henle
*****COULTHARD, J.**
Duo Sonata  BMI Canada
Choose EITHER 1st mov't OR 3rd mov't
**DELIUS, FREDERICK**
Sonata No. 3  Boosey & Hawkes
Choose EITHER 1st mov't OR 2nd mov't
**FAURÉ, G.**
Sonata in A, Op. 13  Kalmus
Choose EITHER 1st mov't OR 4th mov't
**GRIEG, E.**
Sonata No. 1 in F, Op. 8 (1st AND 2nd mov'ts)  Schirmer
Sonata No. 3 in C minor, Op. 45 (1st AND 2nd mov'ts)  Schirmer
**MOZART, W. A.**
Sonata No. 10 in B flat, K. 378 (1st AND 2nd mov'ts)  Schirmer
Sonata No. 16 in E flat, K. 481 (1st AND 2nd mov'ts)  Schirmer
Sonata No. 17 in A, K. 526 (1st AND 2nd mov'ts)  Schirmer
**PAGANINI, N.**
Sonata No. 12 in E minor, Op. 3 (complete)  International
**SCHUMANN, R.**
Sonata in A minor, Op. 105 (1st AND 2nd mov'ts)  Peters
*****VALLERAND, J.**
Sonata for Violin and Piano (1st AND 2nd mov'ts)  CMC
*****WEINZWEIG, J.**
Sonata for Violin and Piano  CMC

### LIST C

*****ARCHER, V.**
Prelude and Allegro  Berandol

**BEETHOVEN, L. VAN**
Romanze in G, Op. 40 (*Romantzen für Violon und Klavier*)  Peters
**DEBUSSY, C. (TRANS. HEIFETZ)**
Golliwogg's Cake-Walk  Fischer
**DVORÁK, A.**
Mazurka, Op. 49 (*Three Pieces for Violin and Piano*)  Schirmer
Slavonic Dance in E minor, No. 2, Op. 46 (ed. Kreisler)  Fischer
(*The Fritz Kreisler Collection, Volume 1*)
*****ECKHARDT-GRAMMATÉ, S.-C.**
*10 Caprices for Solo Violin*  CMC
Choose ANY ONE of Nos. 1. 2. 3
**HUBAY, J.**
Hejre Kati (Czardas Scene), No. 4, Op. 32  Fischer OR Schirmer
*****HYSLOP, R.**
L'Amour de la jeune fille (*Bow Ties*)  Harris
**KROLL, W.**
Banjo and Fiddle  Schirmer
**KREISLER, F.**
*The Fritz Kreisler Collection, Volume 1*  Fischer
Praeludium and Allegro in the style of Pugnani
*The Fritz Kreisler Collection, Volume 2*  Fischer
Choose ANY ONE of
Songs My Mother Taught Me
La Chasse in the style of Cartier
*****KULESHA, G.**
Dark TIme  CMC
**MOZART, W. A. (ARR. KREISLER)**
Rondo from Serenade in D major, K. 250 ("Haffner")  Fischer
(*The Fritz Kreisler Collection, Volume 1*)
**NOVACEK, O.**
Moto Perpetuo  International OR Fischer
**PAGANINI, N.**
Cantabile in D (ed. Ricci)  International
*****PARKER, M.**
In Memoriam  CMC
**RACHMANINOV, S.**
Vocalise, Op. 34, No. 14  Schirmer
(*Two Sentimental Pieces for Violin and Piano*)
**RIES, F.**
La Capricciosa for Violin and Piano  Ries&Erler
**SCARLATTI, A. (ARR. GODOWSKY)**
Gigue – "La Chasse" (*Suite No. 3 in D*)  Bosworth
**SCHUMANN, R. (TRANS. KREISLER)**
Fantasy in C, Op. 131  Fischer
**SUK, J.**
*Four Pieces for Violin and Piano, Op. 17, Volume 1*  Lengnick
Choose ANY ONE of
Quassi Ballata
Appassionata
**WIENIAWSKI, H.**
Caprice in E flat for Violin and Piano, Alla Saltarella  Foley
**VIEUXTEMPS, H. (ED. HUBAY)**
Lamento, Op. 48, No. 18  EMB
**VITALI, T.**
Ciaccona in G minor for Violin and Piano  Fischer

### LIST D

**BACH, J. S.**
Sonata No. 1 in G minor, BWV 1001  Any edition
Choose ANY ONE of
Adagio
Presto
Sonata No. 2 in A minor, BWV 1003  Any edition
Choose ANY ONE of

Andante
Allegro
Sonata No. 3 in C, BWV 1005                    Any edition
Choose ANY ONE of
Adagio
Largo
Partita No. 1 in B minor, BWV 1002             Any edition
Allemande AND Double
Partita No. 3 in E                             Any edition
Choose ANY ONE of
Preludio
Loure
*JOACHIM, O.
Requiem for Solo Violin                        CMC

*KYMLICKA, M.
Partissima for Solo Violin                     CMC
PAGANINI, N.
*60 Variations sur l'air Barucaba pour Violon (solo) Op. 14*   EMB
Choose EITHER (a) OR (b)
(a) No. 24 AND No. 25 AND No. 26 AND No. 29
(b) No. 27 AND No. 28 AND No. 30 AND No. 32
The theme before No. 1 and the "finis" after No. 60 should
be played at the beginning and end of each group of
Variations, in the appropriate keys
WIENIAWSKI, H. (ED. GINGOLD)
*Etudes-Caprices for Violin (solo), Op. 18*    International
No. 4

# Studies

Candidates must be prepared to play TWO contrasting studies in different keys, ONE from Study List A and ONE from Study List B, below. Memorization is recommended although NOT required.

| LIST A | | LIST B | |
|---|---|---|---|
| DONT, J. | | GAVINIES, P. | |
| *Twenty-Four Etudes and Caprices, Op. 35* | Schirmer | *Twenty-Four Etudes for the Violin* | Schirmer |
| Choose ANY ONE of | | Choose ANY ONE Etude | |
| Nos. 19, 20, 21, 22, 23, 24 | | | |

# Orchestral Excerpts

Candidates must be prepared to play ANY of the following orchestral excerpts, one or more of which will be chosen by the Examiner. Candidates should note that for each excerpt, they may be asked to start or stop in the middle of the excerpt passage. All excerpts can be found starting on page 56 of this syllabus. For those candidates who wish to prepare their excerpts from complete orchestral parts, please use the material at the back of this syllabus for reference.

BEETHOVEN, L. VAN
*Leonore Overture No. 3, Op. 72a*
ROSSINI, G.
*Barber of Seville Overture*

SAINT-SAËNS, C.
*Danse Macabre, Op. 40*
SCHUBERT, F.
*Symphony No. 5*

# Supplementary Piece

Candidates must be prepared to play ONE Supplementary Piece. This piece need not be from the Syllabus lists, and may be chosen entirely at the discretion of the teacher and student. It may represent a period or style of piece not already included in the examination program, but which holds special interest for the candidate. The choice must be within the following guidelines:

1) The equivalent level of difficulty of the piece may be at a higher grade level, providing it is within the technical and musical grasp of the candidate.

2) Pieces below the equivalent of Grade 9 level are not acceptable.

3) The piece must be for solo violin (with or without piano accompaniment). Duets and trios are not acceptable.

4) Candidates with exceptional talent for improvisation may wish to improvise on a theme of their choice. In this case, items 1 and 2 (above) will apply. Marks will be given for originality, musical inventiveness, and structural unity.

Special approval is not required for the Supplementary Piece. However, poor suitability of the choice may be reflected in the mark. Memorization is encouraged, although NOT required.

## Technical Tests

All technical tests must be played from memory, evenly, with good tone, secure intonation, with all of the listed bowings, ascending and descending in the keys stated.

### SCALES
*ALL scales to be played from memory, ascending AND descending.*

| | Keys | Octaves | Note Values | M.M. ♩= | Bowings Comments |
|---|---|---|---|---|---|
| Major | all keys | 3 | ♪ | 88 | 12 slurred |
| Melodic Minor | all keys | 3 | ♪ | 88 | 12 slurred |
| Harmonic Minor | all keys | 3 | ♪ | 88 | 12 slurred |
| Chromatic | Start on B♭, D | 3 | ♪ | 88 | 12 slurred |
| Double Stops in 3rds | E♭, F, F♯ <br> e♭, f, f♯ harmonic & melodic | 2 | ♩ | 88 | |
| Double Stops in 6ths | E♭, F, F♯ <br> e♭, f, f♯ harmonic & melodic | 2 | ♩ | 88 | |
| Double Stops in 8ves | E♭, F, F♯ <br> e♭, f, f♯ harmonic & melodic | 2 | ♩ | 88 | |
| Double Stops in 10ths | A | 1 | 𝅗𝅥 | 104 | detaché <br> Start on A and E strings |
| Artificial Harmonics | B♭, B, g harmonic | 2 | ♩ | 88 | |

### ARPEGGIOS
*ALL arpeggios to be played from memory, ascending AND descending. Do NOT repeat the top note.*

| | Keys | Octaves | Note Values | M.M. | Bowings Comments |
|---|---|---|---|---|---|
| Major | all keys | 3 | ♪ | 96 | 3 8ve per bow |
| Minor | all keys | 3 | ♪ | 96 | 3 8ve per bow |
| Dominant 7ths | all keys | 3 | ♪ | 80 | 3 8ve per bow |
| Diminished 7ths | all keys | 3 | ♪ | 80 | 3 8ve per bow |

# Sight Reading

Candidates are required to perform at sight a) a rhythmic exercise and b) a passage of violin score as described below. The candidate will be given a brief period to scan the score, but not to "practise silently" before beginning to play. Candidates must perform each section without counting aloud. It is recommended that candidates maintain a steady beat ,and avoid the unnecessary repetition caused by attempting to correct errors during the performance.

| *a) Rhythm* | *b) Violin Passage* |
|---|---|
| To tap, clap or play on one note (at the candidate's choice) a rhythm in simple or compound time. May include syncopated rhythms, changing meters, irregular meters, and complex patterns. <br><br>Length          4-8 bars <br>Time signature   any simple or compound time <br>Note values     variety of values including ties <br>Rest values      variety of values | To play at sight a melody, about equal in difficulty to pieces of Grade 7 level. <br>Keys           ALL KEYS, Major & Minor <br>Length        16-32 bars |

Example a) Rhythm

# Aural Tests

The candidate will be required:

i)   at the candidate's choice, to play back OR sing back to any vowel, the **lower** part of a two-part phrase in a major key, after the Examiner has:
  - ✓ named the key [up to three sharps or flats]
  - ✓ played the 4-note chord on the tonic [solid form]
  - ✓ played the passage twice.

The parts may begin on ANY note of the tonic chord. Following is the approximate level of difficulty:

ii)   to identify any of the following intervals after each one has been played once by the Examiner in broken form:

**ABOVE a note**
*major and minor 2nd*
*major and minor 3rd*
*perfect 4th*
*augmented 4th (diminished 5th)*
*perfect 5th*
*major and minor 6th*
*major and minor 7th*
*perfect octave*

**BELOW a note**
*major and minor 2nd*
*major and minor 3rd*
*perfect 4th*
*augmented 4th (diminished 5th)*
*perfect 5th*
*major and minor 6th*
*major and minor 7th*
*perfect octave*

iii)   to identify any of the following chords when played once by the Examiner in solid form, and in close position:

*major* and *minor* chords: root position and first or second inversion [to be played in solid form, close position]

*dominant 7th* chords: root position or any inversion [to be played in solid form, close position]

*diminished 7th* chords: root position only [to be played in solid form, open (SATB) position]

iv) to state whether a short piece in *chorale* style is in a *major* or a *minor* key, and whether the final cadences and all internal cadences are **Perfect** (V-I), **Imperfect** (I-V, II-V, IV-V), **Plagal** (IV-I), or **Interrupted/Deceptive** (V-VI). The Examiner will play the passage TWICE; the first time straight through without interruption, the second time stopping at cadence points for the candidate to identify them.

---

# RECITAL ASSESSMENT

Recital Assessments are NOT FOR GRADED CREDIT.

The Recital Assessment is offered in most Practical disciplines, at the following levels:

## I. JUNIOR (Grades 5 to 8)

| | |
|---|---|
| Duration of the recital: | 20 minutes (maximum) of music |
| Registration Fee: | Please consult the current examination application form for the schedule of fees. |
| Prerequisites | None |

## II. SENIOR (Grades 9-10)

| | |
|---|---|
| Duration of the recital : | 30 minutes (maximum) of music |
| Registration Fee: | Please consult the current examination application form for the schedule of fees. |
| Prerequisites | None |

Each level may be taken as many times as desired.

The Recital Assessment takes the form of a short recital that is open to the public, free of charge. It is intended to offer students an alternative to regular graded examinations, and to encourage development of performance skills, including program selection and stage deportment. Its significant benefits include a defined but flexible goal, and the critique of the examiner, an experienced professional musician.

The Recital Assessment does not replace regular graded examinations, but can be a valuable supplement and stimulus to musical studies and repertoire development. The assessment focuses entirely on performance; no testing of technical or aural skills is required.

Repertoire should be chosen from the List Pieces in the Conservatory Syllabus, at or around the candidate's grade level. The program may include a maximum of TWO pieces not on the Syllabus Lists. Irregular list approval is not required for any of your pieces. You may include a maximum of ONE piece using an instrumental obbligato.

The program should be chosen with due regard for artistic and technical style, variety and balance. It is not essential that the recital program include works from every musical period or syllabus list category. Verbal introduction of some or all pieces (though not required), will serve both to demonstrate the candidate's background knowledge and to develop rapport with the audience.

Instrumental and voice candidates must provide their own piano accompanist.

The examiner will give a written assessment of the performance along with a classification of the standard (i.e. distinction, honours, pass, etc.). However, no mark will be given. A Certificate of Participation will be awarded to candidates who achieve the minimum standard of "Pass" or above. The examiner will base the assessment as follows:

| | |
|---|---|
| Choice of program | 10% |
| Stage deportment | 10% |
| Musical performance | 80% |

# TEACHER DEVELOPMENT ASSESSMENT (A)
## Beginner to Grade 5

The Teacher Development Assessment is NOT for Graded Credit and no certificate will be awarded.

| | |
|---|---|
| Length of the Assessment: | 60 minutes |
| Registration Fee: | Please consult the current examination application form for the schedule of fees. |
| Prerequisite | Successful completion of *Grade 8 Practical AND Theory 4* |

Teacher Development assessments are intended for teachers as a preparation to continue their pedagogical studies towards the Associate (Teacher) Diploma level, and also for more experienced teachers who wish to upgrade or consolidate their skills. The assessment is intended to be both a learning experience and an assessment of present skills. It is recommended that before taking this assessment, the candidate should acquire some teaching experience under the guidance of a qualified teacher. Though no certificate is awarded, the candidate will receive a written assessment.

The candidate will be prepared to discuss and demonstrate repertoire, technique and pedagogy for the Beginner to the Grade 5 practical levels, as follows:

### Beginner (approximately 15 minutes)

i)    The importance of how to introduce the child to the instrument.

ii)   How to teach music reading.

iii)  Be familiar with the contents of ANY ONE beginner's book and give your reasons for choosing it. Also, be prepared to explain how to teach each piece in the book, as well as to explain the value of the piece in the learning process. The Examiner will ask detailed questions about ANY THREE pieces, and general questions about another four pieces.

iv)   Be familiar with other beginner's books and/or methods, and be prepared to describe comparatively their differences.

v)    Discuss and demonstrate the value of simple beginning techniques, including how to approach aural training as this level.

### Grades 1 - 5 Repertoire (approximately 30 minutes)

i)    Prepare a complete examination program of pieces, studies, and supplementary piece for EACH grade from 1 to 5, inclusive. Pieces and Studies must be chosen from the Syllabus Lists.

ii)   Be prepared to address issues of performance style, form, composer and period, and also to demonstrate the teaching of technical challenges and musical concepts in each piece.

iii)  Be prepared to perform, at the request of the Examiner, any of the pieces you have chosen. Candidates must provide their own accompanist, if required.

## Grades 1 - 5 Technique and Musicianship (approximately 15 minutes)

i)    The examiner will choose TWO of the following three subjects, Technique, Aural Training, and Sight Reading for detailed discussion, and will touch briefly on the third subject.

ii)    Be prepared to discuss the teaching of memory skills if memory is a standard requirement for your instrument.

iii)    Be prepared to demonstrate any required technique (i.e. scales, arpeggios, etc.) for Grades 1 - 5 as described elsewhere in this Syllabus.

---

# TEACHER DEVELOPMENT ASSESSMENT (B)
## Grades 6 to 8

| | |
|---|---|
| Length of the Assessment: | 75 minutes |
| Registration Fee: | Please consult the current examination application form for the schedule of fees. |
| Prerequisite | Successful completion of **Grade 10 Practical** AND **Theory 6, History 5, and History 6** |

Teacher Development assessments are intended for teachers as a preparation to continue their pedagogical studies towards the Associate (Teacher) Diploma level, and also for more experienced teachers who wish to upgrade or consolidate their skills. The assessment is intended to be both a learning experience and an assessment of present skills. It is recommended that before taking this assessment, the candidate should acquire some teaching experience under the guidance of a qualified teacher. Though no certificate is awarded, the candidate will receive a written assessment.

The candidate will be prepared to discuss and demonstrate repertoire, technique and pedagogy for the Grade 6 to Grade 8 practical levels, as follows:

## Repertoire (approximately 45 minutes)

i)    Prepare a complete examination program of pieces, studies, and supplementary piece for EACH grade from 6 to 8, inclusive. Pieces and Studies must be chosen from the Syllabus Lists. TWO pieces, from any grade or grades, must be by Canadian composers.

ii)    Be prepared to address issues of performance style, form, composer and period, and also to demonstrate the teaching of technical challenges and musical concepts in each piece.

iii)    The Examiner will select at least FOUR Pieces and ONE Study for performance by the candidate, and will ask for detailed descriptions of at least FOUR OTHER works from the candidate's list. Candidates must provide their own accompanist, if required.

iv)    Be prepared to discuss the teaching of memory skills if memory is a standard requirement for your instrument.

## Technique (approximately 10 minutes)

i)    Be prepared to describe and/or to demonstrate any required technique for Grades 6-8 as described elsewhere in this Syllabus. The Examiner will select TWO areas (e.g. scales, arpeggios, etc.) to be discussed in detail, and may ask brief questions about the remaining areas.

ii)    Have an in-depth knowledge of your instrument, including its history, design and mechanics, and also a general knowledge of related instruments.

## Aural Training & Sight Reading (approximately 10 minutes)

Be prepared to discuss and/or demonstrate teaching concepts in the areas of aural training and sight reading. Please bring appropriate materials to the examination.

## Theory (approximately 10 minutes)

i)    Be prepared to discuss the teaching of rudiments and basic harmony, using examples from the prepared repertoire.

ii)    Discuss ways in which you would encourage your students to develop a well-rounded musicianship on their own.

---

# MASS
## in B minor

J. S. BACH

# BRANDENBURG CONCERTO No. 5

J. S. BACH

# SYMPHONY No. 31

**Allegro**

FRANZ JOSEPH HAYDN

# UNFINISHED SYMPHONY

FRANZ SCHUBERT

# BRANDENBURG CONCERTO No. 1

**Allegro moderato**

J. S. BACH

**Allegro**

**POLACCA**

**Excerpt continued on next page…**

# ST. MATTHEW'S PASSION

Arie (Erbarme dich, mein Gott)

J. S. BACH

**Excerpt continued on next page…**

# SYMPHONY No. 101
## ("Clock")

FRANZ JOSEPH HAYDN

**Excerpt continued on next page…**

**Excerpt continued on next page…**

# SYMPHONY No. 38
## ("Prague")

W. A. MOZART, K. 504

# Overture "PROMETHEUS"

Allegro molto con brio

L. VAN BEETHOVEN, Op. 43

# SYMPHONY No. 2

JOHANNES BRAHMS, Op. 73

# SYMPHONY No. 103

FRANZ JOSEPH HAYDN

# Fantasia on a theme by Tallis

RALPH VAUGHAN-WILLIAMS

# OVERTURE "Leonore No. 3"

LUDWIG VAN BEETHOVEN

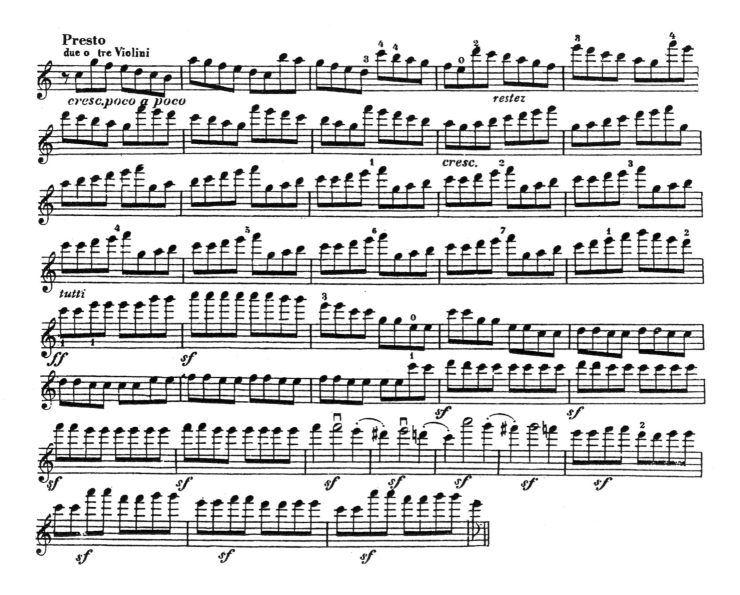

# Overture "The Barber of Seville"

GIOACCHINO ROSSINI

# DANSE MACABRE

**Mouv! modéré de Valse**

C. SAINT-SAENS, Op. 40

**Excerpt continued on next page…**

# SYMPHONY No. 5

FRANZ SCHUBERT